TRANSPORT RESEARCH LABORATORY
Department of Transport

STATE-OF-THE-ART REVIEW 6

THE EFFECTS OF RAPID TRANSIT ON PUBLIC TRANSPORT AND URBAN DEVELOPMENT

by D A Walmsley and K E Perrett

London: HMSO

ISBN 0 11 551133 4

The views expressed in this review are not necessarily those of the Department of Transport

HMSO publications are available from:

HMSO Publications Centre
(Mail, fax and telephone orders only)
PO Box 276, London, SW8 5DT
Telephone orders 071-873 9090
General enquiries 071-873 0011
(queuing system in operation for both numbers)
Fax orders 071-873 8200

HMSO Bookshops
49 High Holborn, London, WC1V 6HB
071-873 0011   Fax 071-873 8200 (counter service only)
258 Broad Street, Birmingham, B1 2HE
021-643 3740   Fax 021-643 6510
Southey House, 33 Wine Street, Bristol, BS1 2BQ
0272 264306   Fax 0272 294515
9–21 Princess Street, Manchester, M60 8AS
061-834 7201   Fax 061-833 0634
16 Arthur Street, Belfast, BT1 4GD
0232 238451   Fax 0232 235401
71 Lothian Road, Edinburgh, EH3 9AZ
031-228 4181   Fax 031-229 2734

HMSO's Accredited Agents
(see Yellow Pages)

And through good booksellers

Contents

Abstract

There has been a revival of interest in Britain in rapid transit systems, especially in the form of light rail or modernised tramways, with proposals being prepared for many cities e.g. Manchester, Sheffield, Leeds, Bristol and Birmingham. Some of these systems may be eligible for government grants towards the capital costs; the Manchester Metrolink and South Yorkshire Supertram have received approval for a 50 per cent government grant. New guidelines for eligibility have recently been published which place a greater emphasis on the contributions which private developers might make towards the cost of the system.

TRRL has undertaken a study of fourteen rapid transit systems in France, the USA and Canada (Marseille, Lyon, Grenoble, Nantes, Lille, Washington, Baltimore, Atlanta, San Diego, Sacramento, Calgary, Edmonton, Toronto and Montreal) to identify the effects which these systems have had on urban development. This report contains a description of each system and its effects on transport and urban development. It then brings the findings together into a set of conclusions and finally considers the relevance of the findings to British proposals in general.

1 Introduction

1.1 The TRRL research programme

TRRL has undertaken a study of urban rapid transit systems which have opened in recent years in other countries, with the principal objective of finding out what effect these systems have had on urban development. The study was carried out because there are proposals for new rapid transit schemes in a number of British cities, and the experience of similar systems abroad is of relevance in assessing these schemes and estimating their effects on urban development. A great deal of information concerning patronage, costs, methods of operation, urban structure and the organisation of public transport in cities abroad has been gathered during the course of the study.

The study has concentrated mainly on France, the USA and Canada, and study visits have been made to the cities listed in Table 1. The visits comprised, where possible, discussions with the transport operators, local authority and town planning agency as well as an extended tour of the public transport system which is essential to an understanding of the city and its network. Discussions were also held with Government Departments and research agencies in these countries.

The reason for the emphasis on urban development is that the cost of major investment in urban public transport infrastructure in this country may be considered for Government grants, made

TABLE 1
RAPID TRANSIT SYSTEMS VISITED DURING THE STUDY

System	Classification
FRANCE	
Marseille	Metro
Lyon	Metro
Lille	Automated rapid transit, underground/elevated
Nantes	Tramway, with some elevated track
Grenoble	Tramway
USA	
Washington	Metro
Baltimore	Metro
Atlanta	Metro
San Diego	Tramway
Sacramento	Tramway
CANADA	
Calgary	Tramway
Edmonton	Tramway, some underground
Toronto	Metro plus tramway
Montreal	Metro

1

under Section 56 of the Transport Act 1968 (and thus known as Section 56 grants). In the case of previous schemes such as the Tyne and Wear Metro, the award of a grant was justified mainly on grounds of time savings to existing passengers and benefits arising from generated trips.

But while some of the proposed British systems may be eligible for government grant towards the capital cost, the guidelines have recently been changed (Dept of Transport 1989), so as to require that all user benefits taken into account in an appraisal are realised through fares, although grant may be payable in respect of benefit to non-users. The new guidelines also place greater emphasis on the involvement of the private sector, not only in terms of building and operating the system, but also in providing some of the funding in return for subsequent development gains. They also take account of the economic regeneration benefit which a project may bring. The potential for new development arising from investment in rapid transit may therefore be a relevant factor in the case for awarding a Section 56 grant.

1.2   Structure of this report

This report describes rapid transit systems in Britain and other countries. It reviews the proposals for rapid transit schemes in Britain, examines the effects of existing systems abroad on public transport and urban development, and for each country describes the policies and regulatory framework which govern investment and funding for public transport.

The report is a compilation of the findings from the study tours, and also includes some material relating to other countries. It also draws on two studies carried out for TRRL by Dr Barry Simpson of Aston University, one being a review of rapid transit systems generally (Simpson B J, 1989), and the other an investigation into costs and methods of funding rail systems (Simpson B J, 1990).

The remainder of this Introduction discusses the renewed interest in rapid transit in Britain and the classification of rapid transit systems.

Section 2 of the report deals with Britain and describes the system of local government, the responsibilities for funding public transport, and the role of the central government. It describes the two rapid transit systems currently operating, in London Docklands and Tyneside, and the four major proposals for new light rail systems (Greater Manchester, South Yorkshire, West Midlands and Avon), as well as listing the other proposals.

Sections 3, 4 and 5 of this report, dealing with France, the USA and Canada respectively, contain detailed studies of the rapid transit systems included in the study tour. Each city is reported under the headings of the urban area, development of the rail system, costs and funding, patronage, and urban development. The information was gained from meetings with operators and planners in each city, site visits and study of reports and surveys from each city. At the end of the section relating to each country, a number of other cities with rapid transit systems are described in less detail, using information obtained from the literature.

Section 6 contains some information about rail systems in other countries, also derived from published literature, principally a study by Simpson for TRRL (Simpson B J, 1989) and a study of Mass Rapid Transit in Developing Countries carried out for the Overseas Unit of TRRL (Halcrow Fox and Associates, 1989).

The remaining sections draw together conclusions from the detailed studies. In this report we do not attempt to summarise matters such as costs and funding or the organisation of transport, except insofar as these touch on patronage and development. They are described for each city separately, and will be dealt with in later reports.

Section 7 summarises the effects of rapid transit on patronage and activities. Section 8 deals with the effects on urban development, and discusses the main conclusions from the study. In Section 9 we highlight some of the lessons which can be drawn for rapid transit systems in Britain.

1.3 The renaissance of rapid transit in Great Britain

Rapid transit systems have been somewhat out of favour in Great Britain over the last decade, probably because it was realised that the technologically-advanced systems proposed during the late 1960s and early 1970s were unacceptably expensive in the economic climate at the end of the 1970s. So, although a few new or reconditioned rail schemes were designed in the early '70s and opened in the late 1970s and early 1980s (Tyne and Wear Metro, Glasgow Argyle Line and Underground, Merseyside Loop and Link, London Jubilee Line), many other schemes were shelved.

More recently, rapid transit has been enjoying something of a renaissance, particularly in the form of light rail, with schemes being considered for most of Britain's larger cities and some smaller ones as well. There are a number of possible reasons for this:

a.   Demand for public transport has grown in some areas over recent years, especially in south-east England, as the economy recovers from the recession of the late 1970s and early 1980s;

b.   Increasing traffic congestion affects buses as well as cars, and has led to a renewed interest in rail-based public transport;

c.   The opening in 1987 of the London Docklands Light Railway has focused attention on light rail - although in fact the DLR serves an area which has many unique features not found in other cities;

d.   The experience of new rapid transit systems in other countries, especially France and North America, has made it a more attractive proposition for British cities, helping to dispel the image of the old-fashioned trams.

Although, as stated earlier, many British cities have proposals for rapid transit systems, most of these are only at the stage of preliminary studies. The plans for Manchester, South Yorkshire, Bristol and the West Midlands have developed the furthest. Manchester has obtained a Government grant of 50 per cent towards the eligible cost and has awarded a single contract to

3

design and build the system and to operate and maintain it for 15 years. South Yorkshire has also obtained approval for a Government grant, and Parliamentary approval has been given for the first lines in West Midlands and Bristol (Advanced Transport for Avon).

There is also a great deal of interest in rapid transit in several other European countries, in North America, and in the Far East. In France, for example, metros have been opened in Marseille (1977), Lyon (1978) and Lille (1983), and tramways in Nantes (1985) and Grenoble (1987). These two tramways in particular have had a strong influence on the proposals for British cities. New rapid transit schemes in Washington, Atlanta, Calgary, Edmonton and other North American cities have also opened during the last decade.

1.4   Classification of rapid transit systems

Urban Rail systems are commonly classified as "heavy", "medium" or "light" systems. These terms refer principally to the type of construction; however, the weight of the vehicle affects the acceleration, gradient and curvature of the track, which in turn affects the average speed and station spacing, and hence the carrying capacity, the headway, and the need for automatic signalling and segregated track. It is these latter qualities which determine the type of transport which a rail system provides.

Simpson (1988) classifies urban rail systems into "Suburban" railways (conventional heavy rail commuter services), "Metros" (traditional, mostly underground, medium weight railways as in Paris), "Light Rail" or LRT (such as the London Docklands Light Railway), and "Tramways" (which includes both traditional city trams and new systems such as that in Grenoble).

There is a wide range of systems which have been described as light rail, from the Tyne and Wear Metro at the "heavy" end of the spectrum (but which uses light-weight vehicles) down to lighter tramways. In this report we shall use the term "Light Rapid Transit" (LRT) or "Light Rail" to cover both Simpson's "Tramway" and "Light Rail" categories. Where appropriate, metros and light rail are collectively referred to as "Rapid Transit".

For traffic control purposes the Department of Transport (1989) identifies three types of light rail operation: LRT1, where the system shares road space with other traffic and pedestrians; LRT2, where the system occupies a reserved space on the road which is, however, accessible to other vehicles during emergencies (like a bus lane); and LRT3, where the track is wholly segregated from other traffic (including pedestrians), although it may follow a highway alignment. The last category is further divided into LRT3a, where vehicles operate on line-of-sight, and LRT3b, where full signalling is used. LRT3b is therefore similar in its operation to a full metro.

On this basis, the London Docklands Light Railway, which has features in common with heavier metro systems, eg automatic control, third rail power and complete segregation, would be classified as LRT3b. The new tramways in Grenoble and Nantes are mostly segregated on highway alignments (LRT3a), with interaction with traffic at junctions and some sections of running in streets and pedestrian areas (LRT 1 and LRT2).

4

In summary, the typical light rail system is light in construction, with station spacing less than 1 km, capacity around 20,000 passengers per hour, and average speed 22-30 km/hour. In many cases it is mainly segregated, but follows a highway alignment; it may also have sections of tunnel, elevated track or street-running.

However, as far as this report is concerned, the classification is to be regarded as a guide rather than a hard and fast division. There are no clear boundaries, and few rapid transit systems fall neatly into one of the above categories. Indeed, it can be said that the distinguishing feature of a light rail system is its ability to span the spectrum from metro to tramway: here running in street, there operating on segregated track at high speed, and elsewhere fitting into the urban fabric with tight curves and steep gradients.

Although the current interest is mostly in modern tramway systems, this report also covers a number of heavier rapid transit systems (metros). This is because the effects of these systems on patronage and urban development can be compared with those of lighter rail systems, and provide important lessons about the probable impacts of new tramways. In particular, the medium term effects on urban development are more clearly identified in the case of the metros, which have mostly been in operation for 10 to 15 years, than in the case of tramways which have opened during the 1980s. Table 1 lists the systems described in this report and how they fit the classification.

2 Rapid transit systems in Great Britain

2.1 Government policies and organisation of public transport

2.1.1 Responsibilities for public transport in Great Britain

In London, public transport is principally the responsibility of London Regional Transport, which is a state-owned body (like British Rail) and is responsible to the national Government through the Secretary of State for Transport.

Outside London, responsibility for public transport policy and funding rests mainly with the local authorities - the County Councils in England (except in the Metropolitan Counties) and in Wales and the Regional Councils in Scotland. The local District or City Councils, in some cases, own a municipal bus operator which, however, is run as a financially-independent Public Transport Company (PTC).

In the Metropolitan Counties (the larger cities in England except for London), public transport policy is the responsibility of the Passenger Transport Authorities (PTAs) and is implemented on their behalf by the Passenger Transport Executives (PTEs). Prior to their abolition in April 1986, the Metropolitan County Councils undertook the functions of the PTAs. The PTAs are now separate bodies comprising Councillors nominated by the constituent districts of the county. In the Strathclyde Region of Scotland (which contains the Glasgow conurbation and also a large rural area), transport is the responsibility of Strathclyde PTE which is responsible to the Regional Council.

Prior to the deregulation of local bus services in 1986, the PTEs operated many of the bus services in their areas. Following deregulation, the bus operations of the PTEs were formed into separate Passenger Transport Companies, wholly owned by, but financially independent of, the PTAs. Some PTCs have recently been privatised.

Before deregulation, local authorities had wide responsibilities for planning public transport in their areas, and the PTEs, in particular, played a very active role in designing extensive, integrated transport systems. Since deregulation, bus operators are free to run commercially any services they wish. Local authorities are able to subsidise additional services as necessary, but must do so by means of a tendering process for individual services, and must not inhibit competition.

2.1.2 Local government funding

For many years, an important source of local government funds was the Rates, a property tax levied on commercial and domestic premises. This was supplemented by the national Government through the Rate Support Grant, which often constituted more than half the total local government income.

In recent years, the national Government has taken powers to reduce spending by local authorities and PTEs by placing direct limits on the amount they can raise through the rates. This power was used for 3 years from April 1986 to limit the overall amount which the PTEs could spend on public transport.

Since April 1990 (April 1989 in Scotland) the Rates have been replaced by the Community Charge, a flat rate tax levied on all adults (subject to certain exemptions). Like the rates, the funds raised from the Community Charge are supplemented by grants from the national Government, in such a way that, provided it remains within a level of spending assessed by the Government according to the needs in its area, each local authority is able to levy a Standard Community Charge.

Local authorities may, if they choose, raise extra funds by levying a higher Community Charge than the standard, though in some cases, the Government has set limits on the amount which can be charged (known as "Charge capping"). Local authorities are not able to raise other taxes such as local income taxes or sales taxes.

Local authorities can spend on capital projects such as the construction of rapid transit systems. In order to finance such schemes, they can raise funds through grants from Central Government, through loans, if the borrowing is authorised by the Government (a process known as Credit Approval), and through the sale of assets such as houses. The cost of financing authorised borrowing, and the funds raised through sales of assets, are taken into account when the Government assesses spending needs.

2.1.3   Responsibilities and funding for rapid transit

The net effect of the foregoing is that responsibility for public transport in Great Britain lies with the local authorities (PTAs in the Metropolitan Counties, and County or Regional Councils elsewhere), but that these authorities are constrained in their powers to raise funds, to subsidise public transport, and to invest in transport infrastructure.

Most local authorities who propose to build rapid transit systems therefore seek funds from other sources in addition to their own resources, such as national Government grants, grants from the European Regional Development Fund, and contributions from the private sector.

Some of the proposed new lines are in areas designated as Development Areas or Enterprise Zones, where planning regulations have been simplified and where grants are available to developers. The proposers hope that new developments will be attracted to these areas.

As a general rule, the national Government expects new rapid transit systems to cover at least their operating costs. Local authorities which propose to subsidise capital costs with the assistance of a Government grant are expected to demonstrate that this represents the cheapest means of securing identified benefits to non-users, so that unfair competition with commercial bus services is avoided. In addition, the operator of a rapid transit system will have no power to coordinate it with the existing transport system; bus operators will be free to integrate or compete as they see fit, although the local authority may be able to subsidise complementary bus services if it wishes.

2.1.4   The role of the government in funding rapid transit

The construction of rapid transit systems requires heavy capital investment, and the revenues received are rarely sufficient to provide an adequate return on the sums invested. This makes them an unattractive proposition for a purely commercial enterprise, but since investment in public transport can produce wider benefits than merely commercial ones, it is usual to request a Government grant. The Department of Transport has powers to allocate funds to rapid transit projects under Section 56 of the Transport Act 1968 (known as "Section 56 Grants").

The Department of Transport has recently revised its guidelines (DTp 1989) for assessing whether a particular scheme should be eligible for grant. Until recently (eg for the Tyne and Wear Metro), grants were allocated on the grounds that a new public transport system provides benefits to travellers and others over and above the fare revenues. The most important benefit was the saving of time by means of faster journeys and the ability to undertake journeys which would not have been made before. In this respect the assessment of benefits was similar to the cost-benefit (COBA) assessment made for road investment schemes.

Under the new guidelines, proposers of a rapid transit scheme are required first to evaluate a set of alternative strategies against a base case or "do-nothing" strategy. These alternatives include traffic management and bus priority measures as a means of increasing capacity, and pricing policies as a means of adjusting demand to the available capacity. If investment in a rapid transit system appears to be a better option, it is then necessary to make an estimate of costs, both capital and operating costs, and to test the sensitivities of these estimates to various assumptions. Estimates of the likely demand, and hence revenues, are also made, using a range of assumptions on fares levels and taking into account the reactions of other operators - a necessary process since bus deregulation, because bus operators act independently and may choose to complement, or compete with, the new rail line.

If the forecast revenues are insufficient to cover costs (including the servicing of loans for capital costs), the guidelines specify a number of courses of action. First, the scope for contributions from developers should be explored, on the grounds that new rail schemes make development more attractive and profitable, and some of these profits should be recouped to help pay for the line. Secondly, the scope for fares increases should be explored, on the grounds that users who obtain a benefit from travelling (time savings etc) should be willing to pay a higher fare.

If these measures prove insufficient, the scheme may be eligible for a Section 56 grant on the grounds of benefits to non-users of the system. Reduction in road congestion is one such benefit. Benefits to non-users could also include potential development benefits in inner city or assisted areas, where a "pump-priming" incentive might induce developers to build in the area. Some of these benefits could be recouped for the tax-payer at a later date through increased corporation taxes, income taxes and VAT arising from the higher level of economic activity.

Therefore, the possibility of a new rail system providing benefits through development of property in the areas which it serves is becoming increasingly important, and many schemes include provision for recouping some of these benefits, by getting developers to contribute directly to the costs of the new system. Another possible method of recouping these benefits, which has been used in the USA, might be to require developers to contribute towards road improvements or provide public goods such as schools and parks as a condition of planning permission. Local authorities in Britain already have powers (under Section 52 of the 1971 Town and Country Planning Act), to do this. Even where the benefits from developments cannot be recouped, they can contribute to the assessment of non-user benefits for the award of a Government grant.

2.1.5   Acts of Parliament

When a new road is planned, there is a standard procedure which often includes the holding of a public inquiry at which opponents can register objections. By contrast, there is no standard procedure for railways. Since, until recently, there had been no new rapid transit proposals for many years, the current legislation (the 1870 Tramways Act and the 1896 Light Railways Act) no longer meets modern requirements. Each of the current proposers, therefore, has found it necessary to apply for a special Act of Parliament to give them powers to acquire land and to operate a railway. This process also gives opponents of the scheme an opportunity to register their objections.

Drafting a Parliamentary Bill is specialised work, and takes many months. The Bill is then submitted to Parliament; this must be done in November each year.

2.2   Rapid transit systems currently operating in Great Britain

2.2.1   The London Docklands Light Railway

The London Docklands Light Railway (DLR) (see Figure 2.1), is a wholly-owned subsidiary of London Regional Transport, and was conceived as part of the plans for the regeneration of the London Docklands. Redevelopment of the Docklands started in 1981 with the formation of the London Docklands Development Corporation (LDDC). The Docklands Rail Study was commissioned by the LDDC in 1981, on realisation that the area was poorly served by public transport and roads, despite being only 2 km from the City of London. Buses were not seen by the LDDC as an adequate permanent solution to the transportation problems of the area.

In September 1982 financial approval was given for the light railway. Royal Assent for two Acts of Parliament was granted in 1984, and the Docklands Light Railway was opened for use by the public in August 1987. The cost of £77 million was jointly financed by the Departments of Transport and the Environment. Of the £77 million, 81 per cent was for construction costs, 10 per cent for management costs and 7 per cent for land costs.

The two lines opened in 1987 extend from Tower Gateway and Stratford to Island Gardens on the Isle of Dogs. There are 16 stations on the 12 km route. Much of the route is elevated, some using former British Rail viaducts. The trains have no driver but there are train captains whose job is to close the doors, which initiates the computer-controlled departure from each station. They also check tickets and assist passengers, and can drive the train manually in an emergency. The number of passenger journeys made on the system was 3.3 million in 1987/8 and 6.6 million in 1988/9 (Department of Transport 1989).

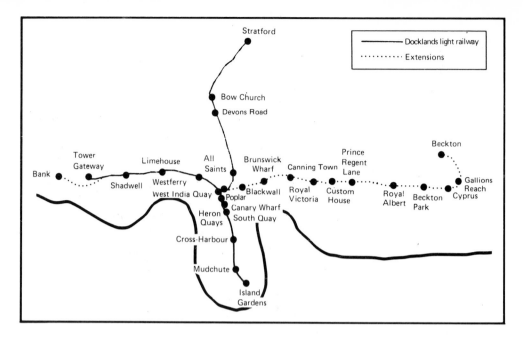

Fig 2.1   London Docklands Light Railway

Major developments at present include a 1.8 km extension to Bank station, financed partly by private funds and currently under construction. An 8 km extension to Beckton is also under construction and is expected to be completed by December 1992. With more cars and higher frequencies this will increase the capacity from the initial design of 2,080 passengers per hour (for the Tower Gateway leg) to 20,000 per hour. Canary Wharf station is being rebuilt as part of a major development by the Olympia and York Company. Further proposals have been published for an extension southwards under the Thames to Greenwich and Lewisham.

2.2.2   Tyne and Wear Metro

Centred on Newcastle, the Metro (see Figure 2.2) serves the Tyneside conurbation, an area with a population of 776000 (excluding Sunderland). It comprises a loop north of the River Tyne extending to North Shields and Whitley Bay, a section from the centre of Newcastle south of the Tyne to Gateshead, Heworth and South Shields, and another section from South Gosforth to Bank Foot which stops 3 km short of the airport. The Metro has 44 stations and is 55 km in total length, 41 km of which is former British Rail suburban railway (mostly at ground level). New construction for the Metro included a bridge across the River Tyne and 6 km of new tunnel in the centres of Newcastle and Gateshead.

The first section from Haymarket in the city centre to Tynemouth was opened in August 1980 and the present network was completed in March 1984. The total construction costs for the scheme up to and including 1986/7 were £284 million at outturn prices (equivalent to £550 million at 1989 prices), of which central government contributed approximately 63 per cent and Tyne and Wear County Council 35 per cent. The European Regional Development Fund

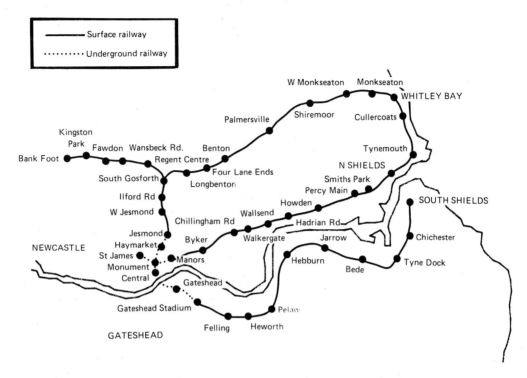

Legend:
— Surface railway
········ Underground railway

W Monkseaton Monkseaton
WHITLEY BAY
Palmersville Shiremoor Cullercoats
Kingston Park
Fawdon Wansbeck Rd. Benton Tynemouth
Bank Foot Regent Centre N SHIELDS
South Gosforth Four Lane Ends Smiths Park
Longbenton Percy Main
Ilford Rd Howden SOUTH SHIELDS
W Jesmond Wallsend
Chillingham Rd Hadrian Rd Chichester
Jesmond Walkergate Jarrow
NEWCASTLE Haymarket Byker
St James Hebburn Tyne Dock
Monument Manors Bede
Central
Gateshead
Gateshead Stadium Pelaw
GATESHEAD Felling Heworth

Fig 2.2   Tyne and Wear Metro

contributed a 30 per cent grant (£9m) to the completion of the South Shields line, amounting to 3 per cent of the total cost.

The Metro was conceived by Tyne and Wear PTE as part of an integrated public transport system including co-ordination with buses in terms of planning, route networks, frequencies, timetables, fares and ticketing, promotion, marketing and development. Through tickets were introduced in December 1980 allowing use of buses and Metro on a single journey. Passengers are able to interchange with British Rail Sprinter trains to Sunderland at Heworth station.

These measures probably caused a considerable revival of public transport usage, with an increase of about 3 per cent per annum in the number of passenger journeys at a time when public transport usage in most other large cities declined considerably, and when population declined and unemployment and car ownership rose. In the year up to April 1986 the Metro carried 55m passengers. Since deregulation of local bus services in 1986, the Metro has experienced competition from direct bus services, but has been able to sustain patronage of around 48m per annum.

Apart from peak periods, journeys to work are only a small part of the total patronage. Shopping is the main purpose and it is in this sector that the Metro seems to have had its most significant effects. As with the new French metros, the city centre has gained from improved access, though this was partly at the expense of small retailers outside the city centre.

B

The introduction of the Tyne and Wear Metro and the integrated network helped to reduce operating costs of the public transport system overall. In 1984/5, the costs of operating the buses had been reduced by about £12.5m per year and British Rail local services by £9.2m, whilst the operating costs of the Metro amounted to £14.9m.

In 1989/90, revenue and other income on the Metro amounted to £16.7m, and operating and administrative costs to £19.9m; thus, the Metro covered 84 per cent of its direct costs.

A contract for the construction of a 3.5 km extension from Bank Foot to the airport, at a total cost of £10.4m (1989 prices), is scheduled to be awarded in March 1990, for completion in late 1991. A contribution of £2.4m will be received from the Newcastle Airport Company. Other extensions, to Washington, Sunderland and Killingworth, are being considered.

2.2.3   Other current rail systems

In addition to the two recent rapid transit systems which are described above, many British cities have traditional suburban rail lines which provide local services. London has an extensive suburban rail network, and also has its metro system (the Underground) with 400 km of track of which about 40 per cent is below ground. Two new Underground lines have opened in the last 20 years and further Underground and suburban lines are planned. Glasgow also has a suburban rail network with underground sections in the city centre, and a 10 km metro (the Underground or Subway, entirely in tunnel), both of which were redeveloped in the late 1970s. Manchester, Liverpool and the West Midlands have a number of suburban rail lines and most other cities have some local rail services.

2.3   Proposals for new rapid transit systems: major schemes

2.3.1   Manchester Metrolink

A particular problem in Manchester (population 2.3m) has been the lack of connection between the two main line railway stations, Victoria and Piccadilly. A number of different schemes for linking these stations have been proposed over the last 15 or 20 years, but changing circumstances have caused each in turn to be abandoned. The solution eventually adopted was a light rail line, mostly using British Rail lines, with a few short but important new on-street sections in the city centre. Light rail avoids the need for substantial renewal investment in the heavy rail lines, while much improving central area penetration.

Six routes radiating from the city centre have been proposed, totalling 97 km (see Figure 2.3). The routes are to Bury, to Rochdale via Oldham, to Glossop and Hadfield, to Marple and Rose Hill, to Altrincham and to East Didsbury. In the city centre tramways will connect Piccadilly and Victoria stations and the network will serve Piccadilly Gardens, the Arndale Shopping Centre and other busy destinations. There will be connections to existing bus and rail interchanges at Bury and Altrincham.

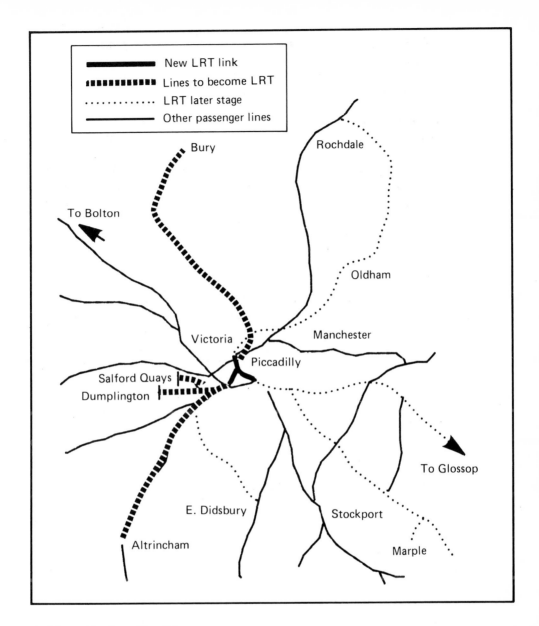

Fig 2.3   Manchester Metrolink

The initial phase, which is due to enter service in autumn 1991, comprises the lines to Bury and Altrincham together with the short city centre on-street connections. The line will be 32 km in length with 25 stations, of which 5 will be in the city centre. Parliamentary Acts giving powers for construction of the city centre sections were granted in 1988. A contract was awarded in October 1989 to the GMA Group (comprising GEC, Mowlem, AMEC and Greater Manchester Buses Ltd) for a complete concession to design, build, operate and maintain for 15 years the initial phase of the network. It is the first time this approach has been used for a local public transport scheme in Britain. The net capital cost of the scheme is about £110m. A 50 per cent Section 56 grant towards the £120m cost has been approved by the central Government; the remainder will be funded by the local authorities under borrowing approvals issued by central Government (and attracting Revenue Support Grant).

Early extensions to the Metrolink system may include links to Salford Quays and Trafford Park (for which Parliamentary Bills have been deposited) and to Rochdale and Oldham. The extensions could be timed to fit in with the phasing of developments planned at Trafford Park and Dumplington, and discussions are taking place with the Urban Development Corporation.

2.3.2   South Yorkshire Supertram

The scheme for a tramway in Sheffield (population 635,000), proposed by South Yorkshire PTE, is different from the other major British schemes in that the first line will follow existing roads rather than using former rail lines. Elsewhere, in the past, this kind of design has been politically difficult; a road-orientated scheme for parts of Birmingham was rejected in 1985 after local protest.

The first line (see Figure 2.4) will extend 22 km from Hillsborough in the north-west of Sheffield to Mosborough in the south-east linking major retail, commercial and leisure developments which are already in existence, under construction, or planned. A Parliamentary Bill for the line received the Royal Assent in 1988, and approval for a Section 56 grant has been obtained. Private capital is being sought to share the financing of the scheme.

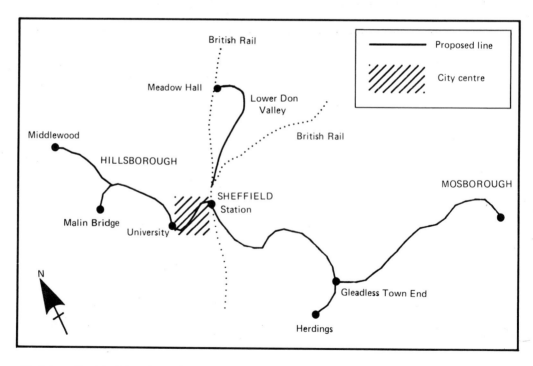

Fig 2.4   South Yorkshire Supertram

14

A second line is planned, following a railway alignment and serving the Lower Don Valley, an area which is scheduled for redevelopment. This route is favoured by the city council, who see potential for development and a source of funding through enhanced land values. A Bill for the line was submitted to Parliament in November 1988.

2.3.3 Midland Metro

A number of corridors have been identified for light rail routes serving the West Midlands conurbation (population 2.3 m). The route for the first line extends 20 km from Snow Hill Station in central Birmingham through the centres of West Bromwich, Wednesbury and Bilston to Wolverhampton (see Figure 2.5). It will use the low level line of the former Great Western Railway, now disused with most of the track removed. Much of this passes through old industrial and residential areas, a considerable amount of it derelict or disused. All the first phase line is segregated from the highway except short sections in Wolverhampton town centre.

It is proposed that the vehicles will be single-deck electrically-operated trams powered from an overhead catenary system and operating in pairs or singly.

The route passes through an area of economic decline. Apart from the termini and the stations in the centres of West Bromwich and Bilston, the majority of the other 25 stations are amidst under-used or unused former industrial land or on the fringe of low density housing, far enough from the main road to Wolverhampton to be inconvenient to passengers. If the local economy does improve however, there is a great deal of land for development along this route.

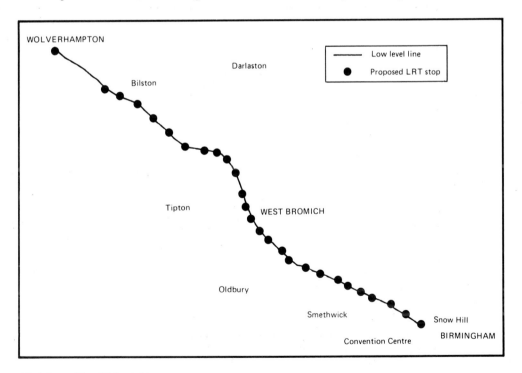

Fig 2.5   West Midlands Metro

15

The cost of the first route is estimated to be about £80 million. It is hoped that the private sector will contribute to the cost in light of the development potential, with the remainder from local authorities and national Government together with European Agencies. Until redevelopment along the line takes place, there seems to be little doubt that patronage on the first line will be low (ridership forecasts predict 5 million passengers per year). It would, however, be relatively easy to install compared with lines in denser populated areas. A Bill for the scheme received Royal Assent in November 1989.

Eventually it is planned that there will be a network of about 150 to 200 km. In the Black Country areas the network could be based on disused or under-used BR lines whilst in Birmingham an alignment mostly on track separated from the highway could be more favourable, either along a central reservation or at one side of the highway.

2.3.4   Advanced Transport For Avon

The proposed tramway scheme for Avon (see Figure 2.6) differs from other British schemes in that it is being proposed and financed primarily by a private sector company, Advanced Transport for Avon.

Several factors have contributed to the need for a rapid transit system in Bristol (urban area population 517,000): poor location of Temple Meads (the main railway station) for local traffic, growth in Northavon and the east Bristol fringe along the M4 corridor, growth potential of Portishead and Portbury, and poor accessibility to south Bristol.

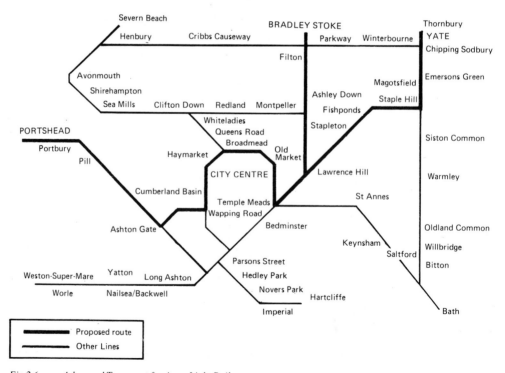

Fig 2.6   Advanced Transport for Avon Light Railway

16

The proposed first phase comprises 60 km of track, mainly following disused British Rail track, with some highway alignment sections. Funding will partly be from land sales at an enhanced value, resulting from the railway's developmental impacts. Some grant may however be sought from central and local government also.

A Bill for the first stage of the line, 17 km between Portishead and Wapping (on the edge of the city centre), received Royal Assent in May 1989. Two further Bills for the remainder of phase 1, 43 km including a section through the city centre, are being promoted.

2.4   Proposals for new rapid transit schemes - other schemes

2.4.1   West Yorkshire

In the late 1970s the West Yorkshire Transportation Study concluded that light rail might be feasible in Leeds (population 445,000), and possible corridors have been protected from development. The West Yorkshire PTE proposed to develop a light rail network from central Leeds largely following highway alignments and making much use of former tramway land. The first line was intended to follow main roads from the city centre before branching out into the eastern suburbs. The total length would be 23 km, over 20 km of which would be separate from road traffic. Total cost would be around £30m.

It was expected that a Bill would be deposited before Parliament in November 1988 for the Leeds scheme. However, the scheme was shelved due to the withdrawal of support from Leeds City Council, which wished to consider alternative proposals.

The Leeds City Council subsequently studied a wide range of light rail technologies and 14 possible corridors, and selected as the best option the BRIWAY Automated Guided Transit system running from Middleton in the south through the city centre and then eastwards to Seacroft. However, this scheme was defeated on the grounds of cost and environmental impact, and currently the City and the PTE are carrying out a city-wide transport review.

In Bradford (population 293,000) there are proposals for a 10 km trolleybus route from the city centre to Buttershaw. By 1993, West Yorkshire Passenger Transport Authority would hope to extend this eastwards to Leeds via Pudsey. The total cost is estimated at £10.2m.

A study of dual-mode trolleybuses under the European Community Programme of Collaboration in Science and Technology (COST) in 1986 supported the introduction of trolleybuses in some situations. This study was a significant part of the PTE's case for a 50 per cent grant from the European Regional Development Fund.

2.4.2   Croydon

Following a study of the potential for rapid transit in several parts of London in 1986, London Regional Transport and British Rail commissioned consultants to investigate the potential of the

Croydon area (population 299,000). Several routes were considered including lines from Wimbledon through West Croydon and East Croydon to New Addington and Elmers End. Other extensions to Sutton, Epsom Downs, Caterham and Beckenham Junction have also been considered.

The study concluded that for an initial three route network, construction costs would be £70 million. The project would involve the conversion and extension of British Rail lines with new low-cost stations, plus a street-running link across the centre of Croydon. The line would carry 18 million passenger journeys each year, and operating revenue would cover direct operating costs and could help repay construction costs.

2.4.3   Southampton

Rapid Transit, a commercial organisation set up within, and wholly owned by, Southampton City Council, has proposed a "People Mover" with 4.4 km of track connecting the railway station, car parks and city centre with the developments which are taking place along the whole of the waterfront, including Ocean Village.

Traditionally, Southampton (population 211,000) has developed along a North-South axis sandwiched between the Itchen and Test rivers, but the new developments are along an East-West axis rendering them difficult to serve by public transport, and too remote for walking. Some of the new developments attract large numbers of visitors but at present cause congestion. It is hoped that with the People Mover more people would either be able to travel to Southampton by British Rail, or at least would be able to park some way away and so ease the congestion.

The proposed railway would be smaller than the London Docklands Light Railway, with two-car trains holding 40-50 people per car. As planned, there would be 12 stops and a headway of 2 minutes, with vehicles remotely controlled. Compulsory purchase would be minimised because most of the route is already owned publicly, by the City or the highway authority.

The City Council is inviting bids from developers for developing the waterfront area, and is hoping to convince them that they should put money into the People Mover, on the grounds that it would give more people access to the new facilities, and will remove the need for car park development. The plan is to fund the scheme commercially and operate at a profit. A Bill for the scheme is currently before Parliament.

2.4.4   Other possible schemes

Various cities and larger towns in Britain are at present considering light rail as one option to solve transportation problems, and/or improve areas of economic decline.

In Glasgow there is an overall transportation study, and public consultation has been carried out on a light rail proposal which would include some street running in the city centre.

In Edinburgh, following a study which compared light rail with various bus options, 6 light rail routes were recommended for construction by 1996. Two initial lines running north-south and east-west with tunnelling and street-running have been selected for public consultation.

In Cardiff a line is proposed from the Central Station to redevelopments at Cardiff Docks, including the conversion of an existing BR line.

In Nottingham a feasibility study has been completed on the corridor to Hucknall and Babbington, which would use some BR track.

In Portsmouth, studies have been made for a Supertram line from Fareham to Portsmouth via Gosport (involving 9.1 km of BR conversion, 1.6 km of street-running, and a new tunnel to Portsmouth), and a 7.6 km street-running line from Southsea to Cosham via Portsmouth.

In Blackpool, some rerouteing and extension to the existing tramway is being considered.

In the county of Cleveland, studies are being made for the conversion of 50 km of BR line from Darlington to Saltburn via Middlesbrough and Stockton.

Other cities where rapid transit is being considered as part of an overall review of transport are Belfast, Cambridge, Chelmsford, Chester, Dundee, Exeter, Gloucester, Liverpool, Norwich, Plymouth, Reading, Stoke-on-Trent, Swansea, and Swindon.

3   Rapid transit systems in France

3.1   Government policies and organisation of public transport

3.1.1   The new rapid transit systems in France

The planning of rapid transit systems in France began in the 1970s when a growth in populations and increasing congestion in cities led to a new interest in public transport. Metro systems were the favoured solutions for the major cities, beginning with Marseille (opened 1977) and Lyon (1978) in addition to an expansion of the Paris railway network. The automatic (VAL - Véhicule Automatique Légère) Metro in Lille opened in 1983. Around 1975, the Government began to consider the best system for medium-sized cities where a metro is too expensive, and as a result a new generation of tramways was developed, starting with Nantes (opened 1985) and Grenoble (1987). Currently, there are proposals for further VAL or tramway systems in Paris, Strasbourg, Toulouse, Bordeaux, and other cities (see Table 2).

3.1.2   Responsibilities for public transport in France

In a typical French provincial city (Paris is organised differently) two bodies are responsible for public transport. First is the Organising Authority (AO - Autorité Organisatrice), a policy-making body with similar functions to a British Passenger Transport Authority. The Organising Authority comprises elected representatives of the communities in the conurbation, and sometimes is a Syndicat Mixte with representatives of the Département as well. The second body is the Operating Agency (Exploitant), usually a private company, responsible for running the transport system either directly or by letting franchises to individual bus companies. In some cases (eg Nantes and Grenoble) the Operating Agency is a Société d'Economie Mixte, a consortium of public and private bodies. In British terms the Operating Agency may be seen as having the planning and operating functions of a pre-deregulation Passenger Transport Executive but with semi-private or arms-length ownership arrangements similar to those of a post-deregulation Passenger Transport Company.

The details of the actual organisations and responsibilities vary. In Lyon, for example, the Metro is planned and constructed by a consortium, SEMALY, but the actual operation is franchised to a private company, SLTC, which is also directly responsible to the AO SYTRAL for running the buses. In Lille, the Operating Agency itself is run under contract by a private firm. In Marseille, by contrast, the functions of Operating Agency and Organising Authority are combined in one body RTM, which is thus akin to a British municipal operator. This is a result of the fact that for historical reasons the Marseille conurbation consists largely of the City of Marseille itself, so there is no need for a joint body of communities. Lille, on the other hand, is a dispersed conurbation of 86 communities, some of them free-standing towns, and has a Community Council (CUDL) which has similar powers to the former British Metropolitan Counties,

TABLE 2
FRENCH RAPID TRANSIT PROJECTS WITH STATE SUPPORT (AS AT APRIL 1989)

1. In Operation:
        Marseille: Metro Lines 1 and 2 (total length 18 km)
        Lyon: Metro Lines A, B, C (total length 14.4 km)
        Lille: VAL Metro Line 1 (13.5 km)
        Lille: Metro Line 1-bis (11.7 km) (opened April 1989)
        Nantes: Tramway Line 1 (10.7 km)
        Grenoble: Tramway Line 1 (8.9 km)

2. Under Construction:
        Lyon: Metro Line D (11 km); expected opening 1990 (now delayed to mid-1991)
        Toulouse: Metro VAL Line A (9.1 km) (1993)
        Grenoble: Tramway Line 2
        Marseille: Extension of Metro Line 1

3. State Aid agreed:
        Strasbourg: Tramway
        Reims: Tramway
        Rouen: Tramway
        Lille: Metro Line 2

4. Being considered for State Aid:
        Marseille: Extensions to Metro Line 2
        Nantes: Tramway Line 2
        Bordeaux: Metro VAL
        St Étienne: Convert existing tramway to reserved track
        Rennes: VAL Metro
        Brest: Tramway

5. Other projects in course of study:
        Montpellier
        Lyon
        Nice

including roads and traffic and urban planning in addition to acting as Organising Authority for public transport.

3.1.3   The French government's role

Public transport in France is the responsibility of the local communities, with input from the Département or Region where their interests are involved. The national government has, however, taken an active role in promoting public transport since the 1960s, when increasing congestion in the centre of cities provoked the studies of fixed-track systems, and has encouraged investment in rapid transit systems by awarding grants. Apart from this, the National Government has a role rather similar to that of the British Government: it sets the regulatory framework, it deals with matters regarding safety and control, and takes an interest in transport planning on a national scale.

However, in normal practice it is the Organising Authorities (AOs) which make the decision to construct a metro or tramway. Apart from its responsibility for awarding grants, the State does not intervene in the local decisions once they have been registered under the legislative and regulatory framework.

3.1.4   Finance

Until recently, it has been Government policy to fund 50 per cent of the infrastructure cost of elevated and ground-level rail systems, and 40 per cent of underground railways, as well as providing finance for investment in road services. At the end of 1987 it was decided to reduce the maximum subsidy to 30 per cent, in view of the limited availability of funds and the growth in the number of proposed systems. Different regulations apply in Paris. Figure 3.1 shows the amount paid in State grants for rapid transit to each city over recent years.

State subsidy is only available for capital costs. The other principal source of public funds for capital costs is Versement Transport, a payroll tax levied on all employers (save the smallest) and earmarked for expenditure on transport. Initially introduced for the Paris region in 1971, it was extended in 1973 so that the Organising Authorities in all large towns (over 100,000 population) can opt to levy the tax, at a maximum rate of 1.5 per cent for conurbations which have decided to invest in transport infrastructure (metro, tramway or major trunk roads) and 1 per cent elsewhere. Smaller towns, of 30,000 to 100,000 population, can levy VT at a rate of 0.5 per cent. Recently the 1.5 per cent limit has been raised to 1.75 per cent, and Lyon at least is considering taking advantage of this increase to aid with the construction of Line D of its Metro. Figure 3.2 shows the source of funds for capital projects over recent years (the data refer to Provincial France, ie all of France outside the Paris Region).

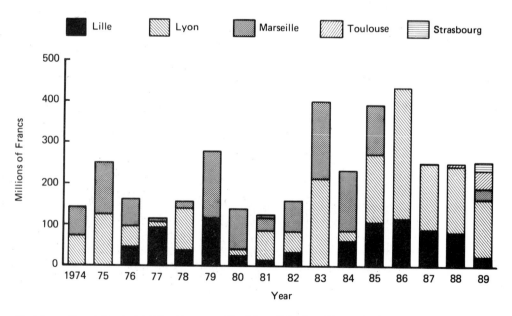

Fig 3.1   French Provincial Urban Transport - Total State Aid to Rapid Transit by City

22

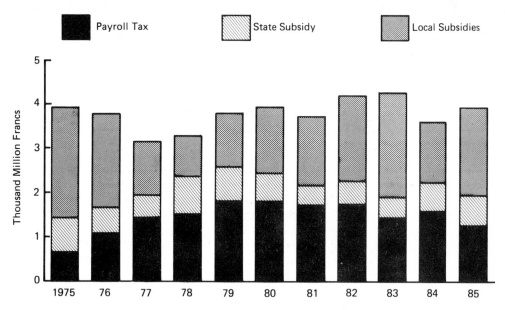

Fig 3.2   French Provincial Urban Transport - Financing of Capital Costs

Public transport in French cities covers typically around 40 to 50 per cent of its operating costs from revenues, which for this purpose include reimbursements for concessionary fares. Versement Transport is an important source of funds for operating costs as well as for capital costs, and has grown rapidly over recent years, as shown in Figure 3.3 (which also covers Provincial France).

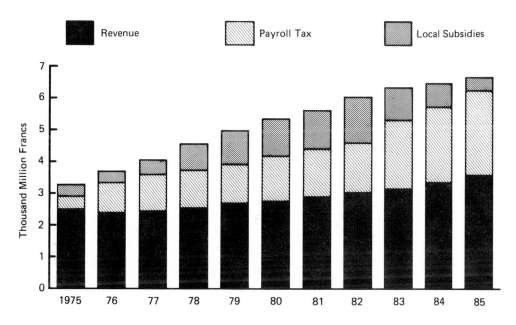

Fig 3.3   French Provincial Urban Transport - Financing of Operating Costs

In most cases, the installation of a metro or tramway has resulted in a greater proportion of the operating costs of the public transport system as a whole being covered from revenue, typically up to around 60 per cent. In Lille, the automatic Metro itself covers 95 per cent of its operating cost - excluding any element of depreciation - since wage payments are very low.

As far as French policies are concerned, the ratio of revenue to operating cost is all important as a measure of efficiency, and increasing the ratio is one of the prime objectives in building a fixed-rail system. The ratio is also a key factor in obtaining Government grants for new buses and equipment.

This ratio of receipts to operating costs is established from the accounts of the companies who operate the transport network. It does not take into account investment charges which, in the great majority of cases, are paid by the AO. In order to develop a more economic approach to the assessment of different heavy infrastructure projects, a methodology which takes into account operating costs, revenues and financing charges is in course of study.

3.1.5   Policies regarding urban development

On the whole, promoting urban development has not been seen as a main objective when investing in fixed-rail transport in France, though it was a secondary objective in Lille and for Line D in Lyon.

Two mechanisms are available for local authorities to influence development. The ZAD (Zone d'Aménagement Différé) is simply a control mechanism to stop speculation; it allows local authorities the right to buy land at a price fixed before the rail system opened. In this way, any betterment value on the land accrues to the local authority rather than to the developer. ZADs have been used only to a limited extent to control speculation, because local authorities do not have the money for large-scale land buying.

The ZAC (Zone d'Aménagement Concerté) is an instrument for promoting development. The local authority buys land for development, draws up an overall plan, and puts in services. It then sells land to developers, so that although each plot is constructed privately, the overall result conforms to the plan. Developers enjoy certain tax and planning advantages.

3.2   Marseille

3.2.1   The urban area

Marseille, the largest city on the Mediterranean coast of France, lies in a geographical basin, on the littoral strip between the sea to the west and the mountains on the other three sides. The city itself has a declining population of 845,000, the conurbation an expanding population of 1.1 m, and there are 300,000 dwellings and 330,000 jobs in the area.

The city of Marseille itself is the dominant community in the conurbation, and the functions of transport Organising Authority and Operating Agency are undertaken by the same organisation, RTM, which thus has the characteristics of a British municipal operator.

It is apparent to the visitor that Marseille is less prosperous than the other French cities studied. Although the traditional maritime industries are declining, there has been some success in developing newer industries such as electronics. Marseille remains one of France's premier cities, a major port and naval base.

3.2.2 The metro

The justification for building the Metro was to improve public transport and travel conditions in the urban area without excessive running costs. Easing the problems of traffic congestion was a major objective, and was the reason for choosing an underground railway, because the city centre is too densely built up to allow any street-level system. The recent availability of funds through Versement Transport was also clearly a factor in the decision, as was strong pressure from local politicians and officers.

The Metro consists of two lines (Figure 3.4), each 9 km long and with 12 stations (two of which, Castellane and the main railway station Gare St Charles are common to both lines). Line 1, from Castellane in the city centre to La Rose in the north-east, opened in 1977, and Line 2, from Bougainville in the north to Ste Marguerite Dromel in the south, opened in stages between 1984 and 1987. Most of the line is underground, with a little elevated track at the outer ends. In order

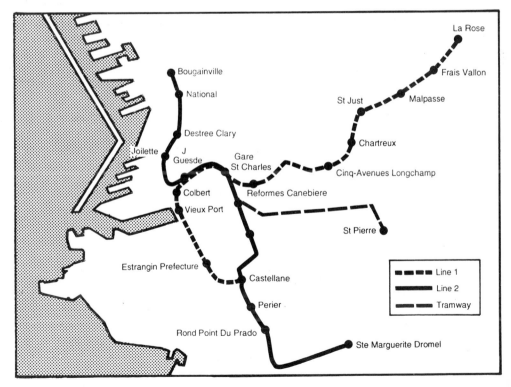

Fig 3.4   Marseille Metro

25

to ease problems of severance, the only ground-level section is the line out to La Rose, which runs in the median of an urban motorway.

The two lines form a circle around the city centre, covering the area between the Vieux Port and the shopping centre, so that nowhere in the centre is more than a few minutes walk from a station.

One line remains of Marseille's former tramway, running from the city centre to St Pierre in the east. This line was renovated in 1984, to coincide with the opening of Line 2 of the Metro, with new vehicles, an interchange station at the inner terminus at Noailles and a bus interchange at the outer end.

More than a quarter of the population lives within 500m of the rail network (Metro and tramway), though the area served is only 12 per cent of the city area. Within 800m lies 20 per cent of the geographical area, but a third of the population and over half the jobs lie within this catchment.

Bus services were reorganised and integrated when the Metro opened, with feeder buses at all stations, except the outer end of Line 1. For Line 2, there are two bus networks which converge on interchange points at Ste Marguerite Dromel and Bougainville. All transport modes in the city have common flat-fare tickets (6.50F per journey, with discounts for carnets and multiride tickets) which allow free interchange.

Further extensions of the two lines are planned. An extension of Line 1, eastwards from Castellane to the local hospital centre is under construction and is due to open in 1992, and firm plans exist for an extension of Line 2 northwards from Bougainville into the poorer housing areas near the docks. Lines have been reserved for further extensions of Line 2 into the more prosperous areas south of Ste Marguerite Dromel.

3.2.3   Costs and funding

The cost of Line 1 was 3000 mFF at 1989 prices. Line 2 was, at 2700 mFF, a little cheaper than Line 1 because the depots and central control room were already there, and also there are two stations in common.

The State Government provided 30 per cent of the capital cost, and the Département 15 per cent. The remainder came from the City, some from direct taxes and some from Versement Transport, which was increased from 1 per cent to 1.5 per cent for the purpose.

Current operating costs on Line 1 of the Metro are 100 mFF/a, and on Line 2, 60 mFF/a. The ratio of revenue to operating cost on the public transport system as a whole is around 55 per cent. With an integrated system, it is difficult to allocate revenues between bus and Metro, so it is not possible to give the ratio of revenue to operating cost for Metro alone.

3.2.4   Patronage

Total boardings ("voyages") on Line 1 of the Metro are 105,000 per day, and on Line 2, 115,000 per day. The two lines together carry 170,000 passengers per day (1987 data), representing 35.5

per cent of the public transport journeys which total 480,000 per day or 159m per annum. This is more than in 1954, when public transport was at its peak, and more than double the number in 1968.

As far as passenger-journeys ("déplacements") are concerned, the number is lower because of interchange, but the 1987 total of 104m represents an increase of over 30 per cent on the 1976 (pre-Metro) figure of 79m. Passenger-journeys increased by 23 per cent with the opening of Line 1, and by 11 per cent when Line 2 opened.

There has been an increase in journeys involving interchange. Bus-Metro interchange has naturally increased, with the introduction of feeder services: 80 per cent of bus routes now serve a Metro station. Car-Metro interchange is well used, with 2000 parking places at park-and-ride stations. Long distance travellers also use the Metro: 2 per cent of the Metro traffic arises from the main railway station, and 1 per cent from the coach station (representing a quarter of all arrivals in Marseille by coach).

Public transport in 1987 supplied 35.8 vehicle-km per inhabitant, as opposed to 26.4 in 1976, an increase of 36 per cent (a similar amount to Lyon). Personal mobility (measured as the average number of journeys per person per day) increased from 0.33 in 1976 to 0.39 in 1988, again similar to the increase found in other French cities with fixed-track systems. The increase in mobility was bigger in the north-east sector of Marseille (Line 1), and average mobility fell in the eastern sector which is not served by the Metro.

The Metro in Marseille is mainly used for obligatory journeys. Surveys on Line 2 in 1984 (when only the central section was open) showed that 58 per cent of journeys overall, and 90 per cent in the morning peak, were for work or education. Journeys between home and work constituted 37 per cent of all journeys on Line 2, compared with 26 per cent of journeys by public transport in 1976 before Metro opened. On Saturdays Metro carries around 60 per cent of its weekday flow, and shopping is an important journey purpose. Most of the increase in travel when the Metro opened was for work and shopping journeys.

15 per cent of Metro users formerly made their journey by car. There was no noticeable reduction in traffic in the city generally following the opening of the Metro, except that along the main roads served by the Metro it was estimated that traffic was a few per cent less.

Metro is seen as serving a different clientele from buses. It has led to a change of image for public transport generally, which is no longer regarded as being just for those who have no choice. Metro passengers comprise fewer females (52 per cent, compared with 62 per cent on bus) and more people of the higher social classes.

3.2.5   Effects on urban development

Although Metro has featured in the land use plans for Marseille published since 1978, there have been no specific measures taken to encourage activity in the vicinity of stations, apart from those which were already in an action zone. As a result, there were no large-scale developments associated with the Metro.

C

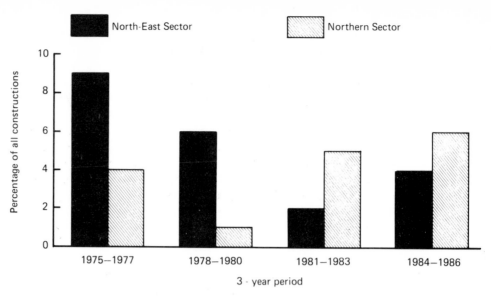

Fig 3.5   Marseille - Construction of dwellings, by sector as percentage of the whole city

Marseille has no system by which to recoup the investment in the Metro. Before it was built, the city authorities thought it would be possible to get private developers to build the Metro, but it proved impossible. Attempts to create ZACs and ZADs near the Metro in order to recoup the investment had little effect.

The benefits obtained from time savings on journeys should be apparent in land values. However, in the first year of Metro there was no detectable difference between prices for housing near to and remote from Metro. These findings were confirmed in a more recent study (quoted in Tulasne 1989) of property values in the periphery of Marseille, where Metro did not emerge as a significant factor.

Tulasne's paper contains some data relating to housing construction in Marseille (see Figure 3.5) which tend to show that construction anticipates the coming of the Metro. Before Line 1 opened in 1976, housing constructions in the north-east sector around the line were 9 per cent of those in the whole city, and were 6 per cent just after opening, but in the early '80s they dropped to 2-4 per cent. In the northern sector around Line 2, on the other hand, constructions were 1-4 per cent of those in the whole city up to 1980, but then rose to 5-6 per cent between 1981 and 1986 (Line 2 opened in 1984).

There are a few examples of development effects indirectly connected with Metro. At the end of Line 1 at La Rose, in the late 1960s there was a programme of development to build collective accommodation and small houses for people returning from North Africa after the Algerian war. The Metro and the urban motorway to La Rose were constructed as part of this comprehensive development. There has been a lot of development around this line since the Metro opened (tower blocks etc), but this is probably more connected with the motorway and with expansion generally than with the Metro specifically. La Rose has now been made into a ZAC.

There are also a few instances where a public development took advantage of the proximity of the Metro, for example:

- a public housing development to the north,
- a new sports stadium at Prado in the south,
- the Dojo Regional Exhibition Hall at Bougainville.
- the Prado Seaside Park which, while not particularly near to the Metro, was constructed on land reclaimed from the sea by dumping spoil from the construction of the Metro.

In addition, it is believed that Metro has boosted the image of Marseille. Tulasne (1989) reports that entering the "Metro Club" has given the people of Marseille a sense of civic pride and of dynamism, of which the clearest result can be found in the development of the city centre. He writes that "the Metro was a determining element in the renewal of the city centre, which involved renovation and rehabilitation projects, the creation of a Faculty of Economic Science, the pedestrianisation of a major commercial artery in the centre, and an increase in investment (including foreign investment)."

Tulasne claims that these major elements of urban policy would not have been fully effective without the Metro to serve the centre. It is difficult to assess the extent to which this is true. During the 1970s and 1980s many cities, both in Britain and in France, experienced rapid development, including renovation and shopping centre developments as in Marseille. In many cities - and this is probably even more the case in France than in Britain - much of this development took place on the periphery of the city. This was largely due to increasing car availability which improved access to out-of-town sites at the same time as contributing to city-centre congestion, from which Marseille, with many narrow streets, suffered (and suffers) particularly badly. The Metro provided an alternative means of access to the city centre, which may have helped it withstand this competition from development on the periphery, so that developments which would have taken place anyway were located in the city centre rather than out-of-town. Geography may also have played a part, in that the availability of land for development on the edge of Marseille is restricted by high ground.

The answer is probably that the Metro in Marseille has aided and speeded up the process of urban renewal which would have been needed anyway, and it influenced decisions on the location of new developments so that they were located in the city centre where otherwise they might have gone elsewhere, but that it was not necessarily the decisive factor in either case.

3.3   Lyon

3.3.1   The urban area

Lyon is the second largest city in France, with a population (1982) of 1.2m, and has been an important regional centre since Roman times. It is situated at the confluence of the Rhône and Saône rivers, and its location has been an important influence on its development. The city centre is located on a peninsula, 7 km long and 1 km wide, between the two rivers. To the west of the Saône and at the north end of the peninsula the land rises steeply, and this has curtailed the development of the city in this direction. The settlements beyond this rise have therefore been geographically separate from the city centre.

These geographical limits have resulted in Lyon being a compact city with a high density of population of around 25,000 people per square km in places, several times the average for British cities. Eighty per cent of the population lives less than 5 km from the city centre.

From the late 1960s until 1980 the city centre was declining, a trend happening all over France with the increase in suburban shopping centres and buying by mail. During the same period the population expanded due to the end of the Algerian war and an influx of immigrants. Most of this expansion took place to the east and south-east of the city.

3.3.2   The metro

The Lyon Metro (Figure 3.6) is an underground light metro similar to the Tyne and Wear Metro. The justification for the Metro system was to create stronger public transport links between the city centre and the new suburbs which were poorly served, and to reduce car congestion. For the more recent lines, planning grounds have featured as a justification, including focusing investment in urban infrastructure.

Line A of the Metro, 9.4 km in length, was opened in 1978. It follows the peninsula from the main line station at Perrache northwards to the Hôtel de Ville, then turns eastwards through the major suburb of Villeurbanne to end on the ring road at Bonnevay. Bus services are integrated, with feeder lines ending at Bonnevay; 2500 buses per day converge on this station, which is also a park-and-ride point. Line B, a short branch through a new commercial centre at Part Dieu, was

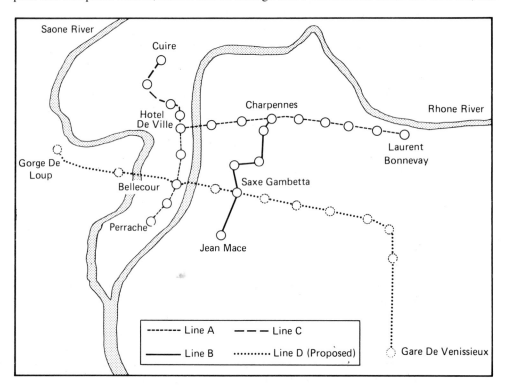

Fig 3.6   Lyon Metro

opened in 1981. Line C, opened in 1984, is another short branch from Hôtel de Ville northwards to the suburbs of Croix Rousse and Cuire; the first part of the line is very steep and the trains are fitted with rack-and-pinion drive. Apart from a short section of Line C, the whole system is underground. The crossing of the Rhône on Line A was achieved by enclosing the Metro in a box section of a road bridge.

Line D, to the south-west of the city centre, is currently under construction. In order to save on operating costs, it will be an automatic Metro, using a system being developed by the Metro Construction Agency SEMALY. Although much of the civil engineering work was complete by mid-1989, development of the automatic system is still continuing and the line is due to open in May or June 1991.

3.3.3   Costs and funding

Lines A, B and C of the Metro together cost 5000 million Francs at current prices, and Line D is expected to cost another 5000 mFF. The main reason for the high cost of Line D is development of the automatic system and its associated software.

For the lines currently in operation, 25 per cent of the total cost was provided by State subsidy (representing 50 per cent of the infrastructure cost). The remainder was from loans at preferential interest rates, which is repaid from Versement Transport levied at 1.5 per cent. Another reason for the high cost of Line D is that preferential loans are no longer available, and commercial rates must be paid. With the high interest rates currently charged, and low wage inflation causing a slowing of the rate of growth of income from Versement transports, it is forecast that in a few years time the income will not cover costs and an increase in the rate of Versement Transport to 1.75 per cent is currently being considered.

Since the Metro opened, the public transport system has covered around 55-60 per cent of its operating costs from revenues, compared with 50 per cent before. The Metro itself is estimated to cover 120-130 per cent of its operating costs since it serves the central areas and busy corridors. The overall subsidy in 1987 was 120 mFF, and has been constant in real terms since then.

It is forecast that after line D opens the ratio of revenue to operating cost will rise to 63 per cent, saving 80 mFF per annum, sufficient to cover the investment costs. A "5th tranche" of the Metro is also planned, which will reduce the subsidy even further.

3.3.4   Patronage

The major effect of the Metro has been to increase accessibility and mobility. There was some reduction in road traffic, but this has since been replaced (though perhaps with a different type of journey, eg less commuters).

The Metro has led to an increase in patronage. On Line A, patronage is currently 4-5 times the level on the bus services which served the corridor previously, and on Line C patronage has increased from 1500 per day before to 15,000 per day soon after opening and 22,000 per day at

31

present. Overall patronage on the Metro is 65m per annum (1987), and 25 per cent of public transport journeys use the Metro.

Public transport boardings ("voyages") overall rose by 55 per cent between 1979 and 1987, and passenger-journeys ("déplacements") by 21 per cent. Some of the increase in boardings is due to interchange between bus and Metro, because a passenger-journey which consists of a bus stage and a Metro stage would count as 2 boardings, but only 1 bus journey before the Metro opened.

The extent of interchange use was an unexpected effect of the Metro. It has been found that people often change to the Metro for only 1 or 2 stations, because they like using it. Surveys show that Metro caters for more men, and more passengers from the higher social classes, than does bus.

3.3.5   Effects on urban development

Business activity in the area served by the Metro has increased over the years since the opening. Surveys by the Chamber of Commerce showed that shopping patterns had changed between 1976 and 1980, with an increase in importance of city-centre shopping which was, to some extent, at the expense of inner suburban shops (Marchand et al, 1983). The extent of the central area itself has also increased - it used to consist of just the peninsula but now also covers the area around Line B, including Part Dieu, an ex-army depot which was redeveloped in 1976 as a business and shopping centre.

The image of the city, of which transport is one aspect, is believed to have improved since the Metro opened. Part of the reason for this is that the opportunity was taken to pedestrianise a number of streets in the busy peninsula area along the line of the Metro, which was not possible before because of the need to allow car access. As a result, it is now possible to walk for several kilometres through attractive, traffic-free streets in the heart of the city. The improved image is believed to reflect on economic activity, especially as far as international opinion is concerned.

As far as urban development is concerned, there have been a number of new developments, some redevelopments, and some reorganisation of space. In most cases it is not possible to attribute these directly to the Metro, though the improved accessibility to the city centre could have been a factor in choosing locations for development.

Line D appears to have had more effect on urban development, even before its opening. The section from Part Dieu to the end of the line at Gare de Vénissieux is a residential and office environment, and in certain locations houses have been bought up and offices built in anticipation during the construction phase of the Metro. In the Gambetta-Grange Blanche area, nearer to the city centre, land has been bought but not redeveloped yet.

The western end of Line D penetrates through the hillside on the west bank of the Saône to the outlying communities at Gorge de Loup and Vaise. As mentioned earlier, this area is cut off from the city, and the opening of the Metro will give a substantial increase in accessibility to the shopping and commercial centre. Adjacent to the station at Gorge de Loup is a former chemical factory site, and an extensive redevelopment is taking place at this point with the construction of new housing. There is also a more general growth of population in this area, and this effect has undoubtedly been influenced by the prospect of the Metro.

3.4 Lille

3.4.1 The urban area

The conurbation of Lille, with a population (1989) of 1.1 million, is the main city of the Nord-Pas de Calais region, and is quite different in character to the other French cities considered here. It is a northern city in every sense that the term is understood in Britain - a polycentric industrial conurbation north of the French coalfield. The conurbation consists of 86 communities of which the city of Lille itself is the largest, but the adjacent towns of Roubaix and Tourcoing, and the new town of Villeneuve d'Ascq, are also important separate settlements. Comparisons with British cities cannot be perfect, but if Marseille is a naval and commercial port like Plymouth, and Lyon is a prosperous commercial city like Bristol, and Grenoble is a scenic, hi-tech university city like Cambridge, then Lille is undoubtedly a regional centre with an industrial hinterland like Leeds (with which it is twinned).

Lille is not constrained geographically like the other French cities; there are no hills or major rivers to hinder its expansion, and even the nearby Belgian border has been no barrier, virtually bisecting the continuous urban area which is Tourcoing on the French side. This could account for the population density being apparently lower than in other French cities, as the city has developed outwards rather than upwards, and traffic congestion appears less of a problem.

3.4.2 The metro

The main justifications for building a metro system in Lille were to improve public transport, relieve congestion, and to serve new developments and improve urban structure. One important objective was to provide a public transport system to serve the new town of Villeneuve d'Ascq and to link it with the main city centre of Lille, particularly since Villeneuve d'Ascq is the location of a major University with 30,000 students. The Community Council decided that trams or buses, even using bus lanes, would not be suitable because of increasing traffic congestion. It was therefore decided to build a fixed track system.

The Lille Metro (Figure 3.7) is a VAL automatic rapid transit system, mostly in tunnel or viaduct. Line 1, 13.5 km long with 18 stations, runs from Villeneuve d'Ascq through the city centre to the Regional Hospital Centre to the south-west. It opened in 1983. Line 1-bis opened in April 1989, running from the main station (Gares) in the city centre to the north-eastern suburbs. At Gares the rails were laid for connection to Line 2. As in Marseille, the two lines form a loop around the city centre, with two interchange stations at Gares and Porte des Postes, thus ensuring good accessibility to all points in the centre.

Line 2 was originally planned as a replacement for the Mongy tramway which links Lille to Roubaix and Tourcoing. However, in November 1989 it was decided to link the development of the public transport network to the arrival of the TGV in Lille. The tramway is to be modernised, with new tracks and vehicles, and it will be connected to the TGV station and terminate at Gares (as at present). Line 1-bis will be extended by 3.5 km to Mons-en-Baroeul, with 6 stations. It will link with the TGV station by September 1993 and the whole line will open in 1994. Later

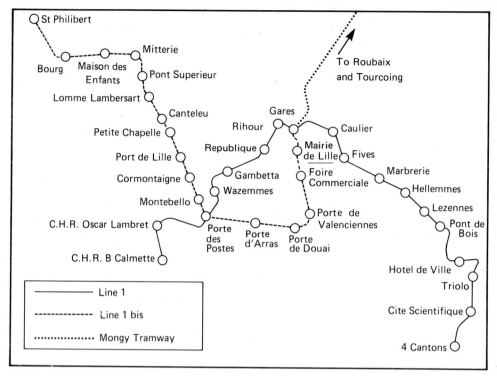

Fig 3.7   Lille Metro

extensions to Roubaix are possible. A separate 10 km VAL line with 15 stations will be built between Roubaix and Tourcoing, and the line is planned for completion in 1995. The VAL line will cost 4800 mFF and the tramway 1100 mFF. State aid of 20 per cent of the cost has been approved. CUDL will finance the remaining cost from loans, to be repaid from Versement Transport (which will be increased from 1.5 to 1.75 per cent) and local taxes (which will increase at 2.4 per cent per annum).

The stations, especially on Line 1-bis where each station had its individual architect, are impressively decorated - partly as an image-enhancing measure, and partly as an aid against vandalism. One city-centre station (République) is built in the style of a Roman amphitheatre where performances are given from time to time. The Metro as a whole is something of a show-piece for MATRA, the company which developed the automatic system, and for French industry generally.

3.4.3   Costs and funding

The cost of Line 1 was 3900 mFF at 1989 prices. This was made up of 20 per cent subsidy from the State (being 50 per cent of the infrastructure cost), 20 per cent from Versement Transport levied at a rate of 1.5 per cent, and the remainder from loans. The loans are to be repaid from Versement Transport. The capital cost does not include research and development costs on the automatic system, which was covered by Government grants to L'EPALE, the Public Office responsible for the development of the new town.

34

The cost of Line 1-bis, which included a new control centre at Gares, was similar, but attracted only 15 per cent State subsidy because other cities also wanted to call on State funds.

The Lille Metro uses only 255 staff for the 2 lines, covering all maintenance and operation. As a result, operating costs are relatively low; in 1989 they were 135 mFF (excluding capital repayments and depreciation), as compared with receipts of 150mFF.

3.4.4   Patronage

The opening of the Metro in Lille caused a large increase in public transport use. In 1983, before Line 1 opened, there were 60m passenger-journeys per annum by public transport; in 1988 there were 95m. Patronage on Line 1 itself was 30m in 1988 - 50 per cent more than was forecast. With the opening in April 1989 of Line 1-bis, the two lines together are expected to carry 50m passengers per annum by the end of 1989.

Surveys after the opening of Line 1 show that 50 per cent of journeys on the Metro were journeys which were not made before. The large generation of journeys is partly due to the turnover of students, who make up half the travellers, and who were poorly served by public transport before the Metro opened. 25 per cent of journeys on the Metro are made by former car users, and 25 per cent by people who did not travel before.

3.4.5   Effects on urban development

The main impacts of the Metro on the city were to cause an acceleration in the developments which were already happening in the more dynamic districts - particularly in the city centre, where growth and development had been occurring for some years, and in the new town area around Hôtel de Ville in Villeneuve d'Ascq, which as a planned development is a special case.

The city authorities believe that, in declining districts such as the Fives-Hellemmes area in the inner suburbs, Metro has had little positive effect, and has possibly even accelerated the decline by enabling people to go somewhere else. The visitor's eye confirms the lack of evidence of any regeneration in this area, which has a generally run-down, boarded-up appearance.

Each station was declared as a ZAD in order to prevent land speculation and uncontrolled development, and to recoup some of the benefit from increased land prices for the city. But in declining areas this had a negative effect by freezing the prices so that owners could not sell their property at a reasonable price. This may have actually prevented redevelopment around stations.

All in all there has been little development around Line 1, much of which runs through inner-city areas, even though five years has elapsed since it opened. There is expected to be little development around Line 1-bis either.

There are more signs of change in the city centre. There are 3 or 4 streets which have been pedestrianised, and extra pedestrian squares around Rihour and République where there was a car park and streets before. It could be that the introduction of the Metro has caused reductions in traffic which have made pedestrianisation possible; conversely, the pedestrianisation may itself have produced a reduction in traffic. The Community Council estimates that there are now 3000 fewer cars in the centre of Lille because of the Metro, though there is no noticeable reduction in traffic and congestion.

3.5 Nantes

3.5.1 The urban area

Nantes lies in the west of France, near the mouth of the River Loire. The conurbation has a total population of 474,000 and consists of 19 communities of which the city of Nantes itself, with 247,000 population, is the biggest. The city centre lies mainly to the north of the Loire; bridges connect it with the Island of Beaulieu and the suburbs on the south of the river, the largest of which is Rezé.

Nantes grew up around traditional maritime trade and industries, especially shipbuilding and repairing. It is, perhaps, the equivalent of the Tyneside area in Great Britain. The main docks and shipyards were to the west of the city centre and on the island. The railway and the original tramway followed the earlier bank of the Loire and together formed a strong boundary to the city, but since the railway was built the Loire has changed its course and there has been an extension of the city southwards on reclaimed land. In recent years the city has seen a period of growth, and traditional industries have given way to "softer" land uses - electronics factories, the development of the university, and the establishment of Nantes as a regional centre.

3.5.2 The tramway

The Nantes tramway proposal was developed in the late '70s and early '80s after the inauguration of SIMAN and SEMITAN, respectively the publicly owned Organising Authority and Operating Agency for public transport in the Nantes conurbation. The availability of funds from Versement Transport, as in other French cities, was also undoubtedly a factor. The new tramway was planned as part of an integrated transport system, with feeder buses to the suburban stations and with areas away from the tramway line being integrated as well with new bus stations, interchange points and articulated buses.

The intention was that with the same number of vehicle-km travelled, it would be possible to offer more seat-km. However, in 1983 a new city council was elected with different policies regarding public transport. The new council insisted that there should be the same number of seat-km on the total system after the tramway opened as before. Corresponding reductions were therefore made in the bus services.

The tramway opened in January 1985, running from the eastern términus at Haluchère via the city centre (Commerce), to Bellevue in the west (Figure 3.8), 10.6 km in length with 22 stations. These termini, plus the intermediate station at Souillarderie and the city centre station Commerce, form bus interchange points. In April 1989 the line was extended northwards by 2 km to the new sports

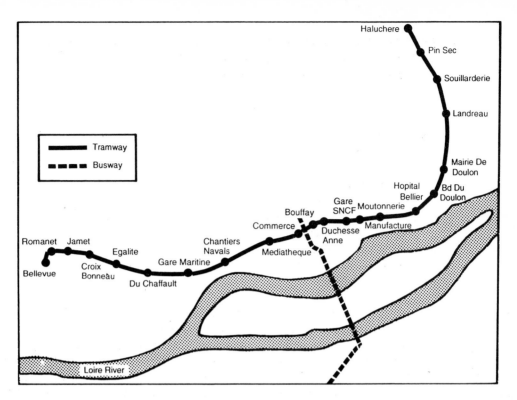

Fig 3.8   Nantes Tramway

stadium at Beaujoire. The opening of the extension coincided with the formal inauguration of the whole tramway by the mayor of Nantes, with a parade of historic tramcars, bands, laser shows, open day at the depot, etc.

A second line of the tramway is planned for opening in 1992, serving the north-south corridor, interlinking with Line 1 at Commerce and crossing the Loire to the suburb of Rezé. The section from Commerce to Rezé has already been served since 1986 by articulated buses operating on a reserved busway (including two new bridges over the Loire); this can readily be converted to a tramway in the future.

3.5.3   Costs and funding

The original section of the tramway from Haluchère to Bellevue cost 590 mFF at current prices. As with other French systems, the State gave a subsidy of 180 mFF to cover 50 per cent of the infrastructure cost; the remainder was financed by loans through the Organising Authority SIMAN, to be repaid over 25 years from revenues and Versement Transport. The extension of Line 1 to Beaujoire cost 53 mFF, with no State subsidy. The rate of Versement Transport was raised to 1.5 per cent to pay for the construction of the line, then subsequently lowered in stages to 1.25 per cent. A further rise in the rate of Versement Transport is contemplated, as a condition of the award of a State grant (at the new rate of 30 per cent) for Line 2.

Since the introduction of the tramway, the ratio of revenue to operating cost for the whole public transport system has risen, from 46 per cent in 1983 to 51 per cent in 1985 and 54 per cent in 1987. In 1987 the total operating cost of the public transport system was 244 mFF (16 per cent higher than in 1984) and the total receipts were 133 mFF (30 per cent higher than in 1984); as a result, the total subsidy, which previously had been rising, has been kept at around its 1984 level.

3.5.4   Patronage

The total number of boardings on the public transport system in 1988 was 69.8 million (after correcting for the effects of a strike), as compared with 51.1 million in 1984, the last full year before the tramway opened. This represents an increase of 37 per cent. Some of the increase, of course, is accounted for by extra boardings as passengers interchange between bus and tram. In terms of passenger-journeys, the number increased from 41.1 million in 1984 to 53.7 million in 1988, an increase of 28 per cent. Before the tramway opened, between 1975 and 1983, passenger-journeys had been increasing at 7 per cent per annum but vehicle-kilometres increased by 11 per cent per annum over the same period. Thus, the tramway has maintained the rate of increase in patronage without an increase in vehicle-kilometres.

A marketing campaign took place when the tramway opened, aimed at young people who were seen as a potential source of public transport users. A "Billet Jeune" ticket offering a considerable fare reduction for young people was introduced, and it is estimated that one third the increase in revenue is attributable to this ticket, the other two thirds to the tramway itself. Certainly, it appears to the visitor that many young people use the tramway, a finding confirmed in an attitude survey carried out by the Town Planning Agency.

3.5.5   Effects on urban development

The older part of the city, near the centre, is composed mostly of apartment blocks. The newer area, outside the ring road, was developed from the 1960s onwards and also has many apartments, but more recently, individual houses have been built, so that nowadays 50 per cent of the population in the conurbation live in houses. Shopping centres for these new developments, and commercial developments around the ring road and along the main radial roads, have been established during the last 20 years - a sign of the city entering a period of growth.

Among the new developments, a number have taken place in the areas served by the tramway. As usual, it is not possible to say with certainty to what extent the existence of the tramway influenced the decision whether, and where, to build the new developments, but it seems likely that the tramway was a contributory factor.

In the Commerce area, the city centre streets have been pedestrianised or restricted to traffic. This makes the centre a pleasant place to walk around, particularly at Commerce where there is a large open square with cafes and shops. Some new shops have been established in the area.

At Manufacture, a kilometre or so to the east of the centre in the area where the tramway borders the railway, the City of Nantes council rehabilitated some old factories ("the tobacco factory") and turned them into offices and public buildings. The area now has a commercial, rather than industrial, environment. An equivalent distance to the west of the city centre, a new arts and literature centre called Médiathèque has been established, with libraries, discos and specialist shops. Other individual developments along the line through the city centre between Médiathèque and Manufacture have taken place, which are gradually turning the area from a rather run-down dock-side road into a pleasant riverside promenade.

Data from the Agence d'Urbanisme (Town Planning Agency) in Nantes show how planning permissions for residences (Permis de Construire) have increased over recent years. Between 1983 and 1986 the number of permissions granted over the whole of the conurbation remained fairly constant, while there was a rise of 40 per cent in the inner area (consisting of the City of Nantes and the community of St Herblain). Along the tramway corridor (within 400m of the line), however, there was a very significant sharp increase from 153 permissions in 1983 to 528 in 1986, a factor of 3.4. These changes are illustrated in Figure 3.9.

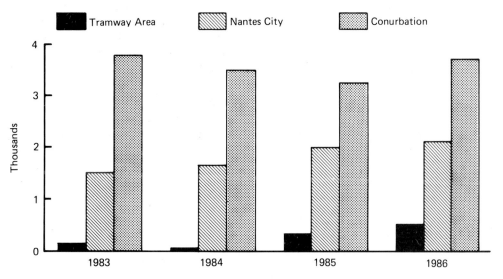

Fig 3.9   Nantes - Construction Permits for Dwellings

Closer inspection of the data reveals that the sharp rise was caused more by a small number - 6 or 7 - of large developments near to the tramway rather than many individual permissions. Some of these larger developments are to the east of the city on green field sites - ie in the area where the city would expand naturally whether the tramway was there or not. Figure 3.10 shows the distribution of developments by size, and demonstrates that in the tramway corridor there were more large developments than in the city generally (this difference, however, is of low statistical significance). Records of parcels of land put on the market also show strong increases in the area of the tramway, both in terms of numbers of sales and area of land sold. Data on authorisations and sales of offices and commercial developments show strong increases in all areas, with slightly fewer in the tramway area. Shopping authorisations in the tramway corridor in particular showed a fall in 1986, following the opening of the tramway. However, the shop and office data are strongly influenced by the phasing of individual developments so identifying a trend is not easy.

The conclusion is that there is positive evidence that housing developments took place preferentially in the tramway corridor following the opening, though it cannot be said that these

Type of dwelling

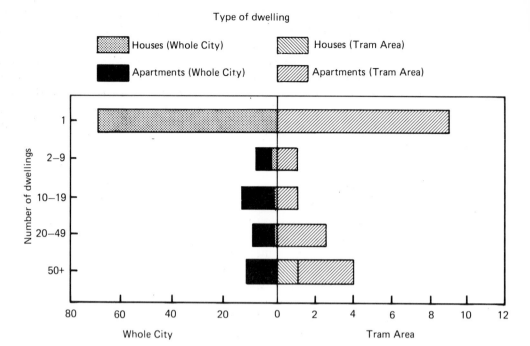

Fig 3.10   *Nantes - Construction Permits 1986 No of Permits by size of development*

were definitely due to the tramway itself. There was no strong evidence of an effect of the tramway on office and shop developments.

3.6   Grenoble

3.6.1   The urban area

Grenoble is the chief town of the Département of Isère in the Dauphiné region of the French Alps. The city itself has a population of about 160,000 and the whole conurbation, which consists of 32 communities, has a population of 391,000. Grenoble lies at the junction of the Drac and Isère rivers, and is located in a valley between mountains. Only on the south side of the conurbation, in the outer communities, is there scope for expansion.

The region depends on traditional industries such as sheep-farming and forestry. Grenoble itself, however, has developed rapidly since the 1960s and has become known as a hi-tech city, a centre for electronics and nuclear research, and an important university city. The driving force behind this rapid development was the mayor, Hubert Dubedout, who made Grenoble a "pilot town" for experiments of all kinds - artistic and social as well as technological. The decision to build a tramway system in Grenoble was made under M Dubedout's administration, and though he was replaced in 1983 by the more conservative M Carignon, the project was by then well-advanced, and a referendum confirmed the decision.

40

It is interesting to note that under the French system of Government, the mayor of a major city like Grenoble personally has much more influence than is the case in Britain. Part of the reason for this is that Government Ministers are not Members of the National Assembly; they therefore tend to make their name through local politics more than in Britain, and it is not unusual for a Mayor to hold Government office as well (the current Mayor of Grenoble was Minister for the Environment from 1986-88 in the Chirac government, and the Mayor of Paris is a former Prime Minister). The influence of the local Mayor was an important factor in the investment in the Nantes tramway also, and in the recent decision in Strasbourg to proceed with a tramway rather than a VAL metro system.

3.6.2   The tramway

The justifications for building a tramway system were to improve public transport and ease overloading of buses, to arrest operating subsidies, improve productivity and reduce operating costs, and to reduce the nuisance caused by over 60 buses per hour using the southern corridor. Improving the image of Grenoble, as with many of the projects described above, also featured as an objective. The tramway system was seen as the backbone of the public transport network which has been restructured around it. The reasons for preferring a tramway were that demand and population density were not high enough to support a metro in a small city such as Grenoble, and also that the ground was unsuitable for tunnelling.

One of the objectives in designing the tramway was to make it accessible to elderly and disabled people; the handicapped associations in Grenoble were instrumental in supporting the tramway at the time of the referendum. For this reason, it was decided to develop a new design of low-floored vehicle which would be more accessible than the vehicle used on the Nantes system which had opened a year or two earlier. The Grenoble tramcar has its electronics and control equipment built into the roof, leaving room for a low (30 cm) floor. This floor extends most of the length of the tram, through axle-less trailer bogies in the centre of the vehicle, and only rises to a higher level over the tractor bogies at the ends of the car. Platforms are correspondingly low, and have been constructed as part of the street pavements with barely-perceptible slopes.

The tramway (Figure 3.11) is operated by SEMITAG and opened in 1987, with 8.8 km of line and 22 stations. The line is at ground level; in the suburbs it runs mostly alongside the highway but separated from the traffic, and it runs through the streets in the city centre. The City council took the opportunity to pedestrianise much of the city centre when the tramway opened.

The line starts at Grand' Place, a shopping development, bus interchange and car park on the southern edge of the city, close to a large exhibition centre (Alpexpo). It runs northwards into the city along a major highway, then threads its way through the city centre mainly in pedestrianised streets. It then serves the main railway station before turning westwards, crossing the river Drac, and entering the adjacent town of Fontaine. In the narrow streets of Fontaine the tram has priority; sometimes the street is reserved for the tram, sometimes, where it is wide enough, there is one line of traffic. Interestingly, traffic appears to respect the reserved track which is protected only by white-lining, whereas along the tramway route in Marseille - a much wider street - traffic appears to use the whole width of the street freely except when there is actually a tramcar there.

A second line of the tramway, 5.8 km long, is under construction and is scheduled to open in

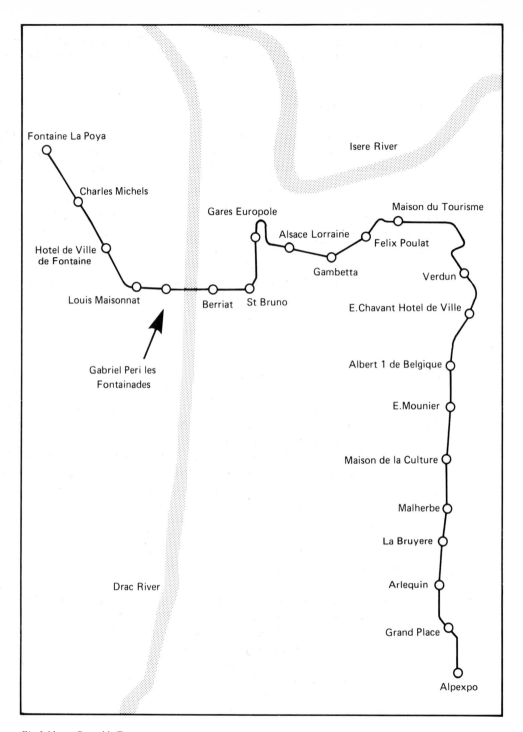

Fig 3.11   Grenoble Tramway

42

December 1990. It will share some of the city centre route from the station with Line 1 but then will branch eastwards to serve the University, involving a double crossing of the Isère.

3.6.3   Costs and funding

The total cost of the system was 1020 mFF at 1985 prices, of which the state contributed 390 mFF (38 per cent), being 50 per cent of the infrastructure cost plus a contribution towards noise reduction and environmental improvements. The remaining cost was financed from loans to be repaid from versement transport.

Before the tramway opened the ratio of revenue to operating cost on the public transport system was around 40-45 per cent. Following the opening of the tramway, by April 1989 this ratio had risen to 52 per cent, and was expected to reach 58-59 per cent with the opening of Line 2. As a result of the tramway, the network provides more seat-miles with fewer vehicles and fewer employees; this is an important factor in reducing cost, as 70 per cent of the operating cost is accounted for by wages.

3.6.4   Patronage

It was forecast that total annual public transport usage would increase from 38m to 45m (18 per cent) following the opening of the tramway. It did in fact rise by 15 per cent to around 40m per annum, but traffic was depressed during construction, so the rise from the level of several years previously (37m) was not so large as forecast. Ridership on the tramway itself is 55,000 to 60,000 per day (equivalent to about 18m pa.). Traffic in the corridor served by the tramway increased 1.5-2 times over its previous level, though where 46 buses per hour had been required in this corridor before, there are only 16 trams per hour now. The frequency on the tramway has gradually been increased from every 10 minutes soon after opening to every 4 minutes from September 1989, when extra vehicles were introduced.

The tramway is very heavily used in the evenings, serving as it does the city centre with shops, theatres and cinemas. The tramway runs until after midnight and is still busy even then, although most of the connecting buses cease at 21:30.

Surveys show that half the passengers on the tramway interchange with bus. Many passengers also travel to the tramway by car. Surveys were carried out at Grand' Place and at 5 stations in Fontaine where parking is available in the immediate vicinity, and these showed that around 5 per cent of the passengers boarding at these stations on a weekday, and around 10 per cent on a Saturday, parked their cars nearby, with another 2-4 per cent being given a lift to the station. The vast majority of these travellers go to the city centre, and half of them on a weekday, and 90 per cent on Saturday, are going shopping. Up to three-quarters of these passengers would have travelled by car if the tramway had not been available.

D

3.6.5   Effects on urban development

In the 1960s Grenoble had an urban plan which created a Green Belt in order to prevent urban sprawl spreading up the valleys; this had the effect of concentrating development in the existing urban centres. In addition, height restrictions were used as a planning control which were more generous for larger developments. These moves were designed to make the city easier to serve by public transport.

There are three main effects of the tramway in the field of urban development. One is, as mentioned above, that as part of the installation of the tramway, the city centre was extensively pedestrianised, including both narrow winding streets where shop fronts had to be moved back to allow room for the tramway, and wide boulevards which have become major pedestrian thoroughfares served by the tramway but with room for pedestrians to wander around the shops and sit at cafes. These moves have made the city centre a very attractive place to visit and shop. Before the tramway opened, there were fears among shopkeepers that they would lose trade as a result of customers no longer being able to park right outside the shop door, but in the event these fears have not materialised and most people now consider the changes to be for the better. It is reported that some new shops have opened as a result of the tramway, including two develop-ments in Fontaine as described below.

The second effect is the redevelopment of old railway yards near to the station as an office, hotel and factory centre called Europole. It was hoped that the site would attract major companies to base their headquarters in Grenoble, but in the event it is used more by local companies relocating to a more central site. Although Europole is close to the tramway, it is not very well served, and the coming of the tramway was probably only a minor factor (if a factor at all) in the decision to develop there; the coming of the TGV to Grenoble and the proximity of major motorways were more important.

The third effect was that in the town of Fontaine the planning of the tramway offered an opportunity for redeveloping the 19th century town centre, as an alternative to locating the tramway in the back streets which would have caused less change but would have made the tramway less effective. Since little money for redevelopment was available from the Département, the Transport authority SMTC provided money as part of the construction cost of the tramway. A number of apartment blocks and other developments are being constructed around the tramway line by the organisation HLM, a housing association which provides accommodation at moderate rents. These include commercial and housing developments at Joliot-Curie (1200 square metres of commercial space plus 80 dwellings) and at Gabriel-Peri (950 square metres of commercial space plus some housing).

Extensions to the tramway line may lead to further development. One possible route for Line 3 is from the station northwards via Europole to the CNRS nuclear research site. This could lead to further development at Europole, but the nuclear site, being neither a tourist attraction nor a large employer, is unlikely to have much effect. A second possibility is a southwards extension from Grand' Place and Alpexpo through the industrial park to a new interchange with the proposed suburban railway, then across the motorway through currently under-used land to the urban centre at Echirolles. This line would show a good deal of potential for development as it is to the south that the natural area of expansion of the city already lies.

44

The Town Planning Agency (AURG) in Grenoble is conducting a study of the effects of the tramway on shopping, housing and population trends. The study will continue for several years as these effects are long-term. An interim report is expected in 1991.

3.7   Other French cities

3.7.1   Paris

Paris is, of course, by far the largest city in France, with a population of 2m in the City and 10m in the region, and in most aspects, including organisation and financing of transport, it is very different from other French cities. There is a 5000 mFF 5 year plan for investment in Métro and railways, with 7000 mFF allocated for the next 5 years. National government provides 70 per cent of the operating subsidy for transport in Paris, with the remainder from the Départements in the Ile de France region and the City of Paris.

RATP, the Parisian transport authority, is to build a tramway line in the suburbs of Paris to connect the Métro termini at St Denis and Bobigny (IRJ 1985). The line is 9.1 km long and runs on a reserved track alongside the highway, but segregated from traffic except at road junctions. The vehicles are to be the low-floor design used in Grenoble.

The objectives of the tramway are to increase public transport use in the suburbs, to connect the suburban centres of St Denis, Courneuve and Bobigny, and to assist in the revitalisation of St Denis where an old industrial area is being replaced by a pedestrianised commercial centre.

The line is due to open in 1992. It is expected to cost 800 mFF, of which 600 mFF is for infrastructure and 200 mFF for rolling stock. Funding is to be 50 per cent from the State, 42.8 per cent from the Region Ile de France, and 7.2 per cent from the Département - the latter representing the excess cost of trams over buses.

3.7.2   Strasbourg

The local council in Strasbourg (population 372,000) has recently made the decision to build a tramway system similar to that in Grenoble (Aufresne, 1989). The plans will be put to a public consultation in October 1990. As planned, the tramway will be 30 km long, thus avoiding too many interchanges which would be necessary with a shorter system. The line is estimated to cost 2500-3000 mFF, and will require a 1 per cent increase in local taxation. The Bas-Rhin Département and the Alsace region will contribute to the cost, and State grants have recently been agreed. Work is planned to start in 1991, and the first phase of the tramway will enter service in mid-1994.

Originally, it was planned to install a VAL automatic metro system like the one in Lille. This was to be 18 km long and would cost 4200 mFF. Supporters of the VAL system have pointed out that it would cause less disruption to traffic, both in construction and in operation, and would provide a faster journey time. The decision to opt for a tramway is recent, following local elections at which investment in transport was an issue. It was made on grounds of cost, of urban development, and of a tramway being more suitable to the structure of the city.

3.7.3   Toulouse

Line A of the Toulouse (population 538,000) Metro, a VAL system, is under construction and is due to open in July 1993. It is 9.7km long with 15 stations, and has 5.8km of bored tunnel and 1.1km of cut-and-cover tunnel.

Line B will be 7.9 km long. Line C is to be an upgraded SNCF commuter line from the main Matabiau station (IRJ 1989, RGI 1985). The total cost of lines A and B is estimated at 3400 mFF, of which 550 mFF will come from State grant. The decision to build a VAL instead of a tramway, which would have cost 1300 mFF, was a narrow one taken by the Organising Authority on a casting vote.

3.7.4   Bordeaux, Rennes and Montpellier

Studies are under way for a 11.4 km VAL system in Bordeaux (population 637,000) costing 3600 mFF and for a 13 km VAL line in the longer term in Montpellier (IRJ 1986). Rennes has decided to build the first line of a VAL system, at a cost of 2000 mFF.

3.7.5   Reims, Rouen, Brest, St Etienne

An upgrading of the tram system is planned in St Etienne, the only French city which kept a full tram network when others abandoned theirs (apart from the individual lines in Lille and Marseille) in the 1950s. A new depot and a 2km extension beyond Terrasse will be opened in 1991, and 15 low-floor articulated vehicles will be put in service.

Reims plans a 7.4 km tramway line extending southwards from the city centre at an estimated cost of 775 mFF (Simpson 1990) with assistance from a State grant which has been agreed in principle. New tramway systems along the Grenoble and Nantes models are also being considered in Brest (with 2 lines totalling 11 km at a cost of 780 mFF), and Rouen (where a State grant has been agreed in principle). (IRJ 1986).

3.8   Some conclusions on the effects of rapid transit in France

Many of the effects of rapid transit in France are similar to those found in other countries, differing perhaps in scale or degree. These conclusions will be discussed in a later section of the report. Here, we highlight some factors which have influenced the development of rapid transit which depend on the particular circumstances in France.

3.8.1 Commitment to public transport

In France, public transport is seen as a public service, and commitment to it is high. The major objective for the development of rapid transit systems in France is to improve public transport - in other words to provide a faster, more reliable, greater capacity transport system than can be provided by buses alone. In order to maximise the use of the rail system, transport is integrated, with feeder buses serving metro or tramway stations, and a common flat-fare ticketing system. These transport objectives are often coupled with the objectives of providing an alternative to congested roads, and even of reducing congestion itself.

Although there are other objectives for developing rapid transit in France, such as improving business activity, improving the image of the city, and providing a spur for urban development, these are usually secondary to improving public transport.

One major way in which this commitment to public transport manifests itself is in the relatively high (by British standards) level of subsidy which is tolerated; a ratio of revenue to operating cost on the whole public transport network of 60 per cent is considered good, 50 per cent is typical, and lower ratios not unusual.

Another facet is the importance of the ratio of revenue to operating cost itself as an estimate of efficiency. Many transport operators have as a major objective the maximisation of this ratio, rather than a commitment to reduce subsidy as an absolute amount. Some transport systems have in fact achieved a reduction in the actual level of subsidy by installing a rapid transit system, but in France it is regarded as a good thing if the new system achieves a higher proportion of costs covered from revenues even if the actual subsidy increases.

Services in the large cities in France are centrally planned in much the same way as they were in British PTEs before deregulation, and transport services in the cities are fully integrated. However, French transport in general is not publicly owned. On the contrary, France has achieved an interesting mixture of central planning and private operation of transport. Most bus operators and some metro operators in France are privately owned, and in many cases the Organising Authority itself is a consortium of public and private interests. Traditionally, a private company has operated the transport under a management contract, with the Organising Authority taking the risk if receipts did not match the forecasts. More recently, "prix forfaitaire" contracts under which the operator keeps part of the profits, or accepts part of the loss, have become more common.

3.8.2 The effect of the urban structure

In some respects, the structure of French cities lends itself to metro and public transport. Population densities are around twice as high in French cities as in British cities of equivalent size. This is mainly due to the French tradition of living in apartments rather than in individual houses; this greatly increases the number of people who live within walking distance of a metro station and leads to the development of compact cities. The apartment tradition is slowly being eroded, as seen in Nantes where most of the newer suburbs on the outskirts of the city consist of individual housing.

Several of the cities with metros also have geographical barriers to movement and development in the form of rivers and mountains, and these too have caused the cities to develop upwards rather than outwards. Few British cities are close to hills which limit development.

3.8.3   The importance of political structure

In France the system of government tends to favour decision making at a local level, with the powers of local government being defined in the Constitution rather than, as in Britain, being devolved by Parliament and subject to periodic change. Formerly, the local authority's plans for a rapid transit system had to be approved by the Prefect (the local representative of the national government), to ensure that the proper procedures had been followed, including public consultation; this was the procedure in the case of the Lyon and Marseille metros. Following local government reforms in the 1980s, the powers of the Prefect have passed to Regional and Departemental Councils. As a result, the decision to proceed with the construction of a rapid transit system lies at the local level. The personal influence of the Mayor in the decision to build a rapid transit system in several cities has already been noted, and indeed the French Mayor generally has more power than his British counterpart, being both party leader and chief executive.

The availability of funds is, of course, also a determining factor. The French government has taken an active role in promoting public transport, and while its policy is to reduce state subsidies, it also believes in improving public transport by investment in rapid transit systems, and encourages this by awarding grants. Versement transport is also important as a predictable source of income, as has already been noted, and this has also enabled schemes to proceed with the assurance of a steady source of funds.

3.8.4   The effect of the planning process

Local authorities in France are more actively involved in planning through the development of local plans and development initiatives than is the case in Britain, where local authorities tend to have a reactive role. Coupled with the municipality's role as transport Organising Authority as well as planning authority, this should favour the process of planning rapid transit as part of a comprehensive development, in a way which only occurs in Enterprise Zones such as Docklands in Britain.

Indeed, in making the decision to build a tramway which is mostly at ground level, it is necessary to take into account how it will be inserted into the urban fabric, and this requires a plan which involves both transport and urban planning considerations. This is less evident for a metro or a VAL project which is mostly in tunnel or viaduct.

48

4 Rapid transit systems in the USA

4.1 Federal policies for funding rail investment in the USA

Capital funding for transit investment in the United States comes from three main sources - the local community, the state and federal funding. Local communities may decide to build and operate new rapid transit systems without Federal approval or financial assistance, though they may require approval from the State authorities.

However, most communities require some federal grant aid for rapid transit investment and so the Urban Mass Transportation Administration (UMTA) has an elaborate process for dealing with grant applications. UMTA assesses the eligibility of projects according to specific criteria and makes recommendations to Congress concerning grants. The final decision on grant aiding is political and sometimes contrary to UMTA recommendations.

Local transit receives approximately $3 billion in federal support each year. Of this, $1.2 billion is contained in a discretionary programme, the rest being allocated by formula. About $400 million is reserved for the development of the twelve oldest systems (i.e. New York, Boston, Pittsburgh etc.). Another $350 million is allocated to maintaining existing transit systems and the remaining $450 million is allocated for investment in new fixed guideway systems.

In an effort to ensure that discretionary capital grants would go only to the best transit investments, UMTA adopted its Major Capital Investment Policy in May 1984. The policy formalises UMTA's procedures for reviewing applications for grants. It specifies the criteria to be used in rating the projects for their cost effectiveness and the stability and reliability of the local financial commitment.

Currently, urbanised areas seeking funds for major capital projects are required to conduct a Systems Planning study, which identifies high priority corridors in the area and explores possible options for improving services in those corridors. This study must also examine the financial capacity of the area in order to realistically determine the future funding available for construction and operation of new capital projects in addition to the operation and proper maintenance of the current system. If, at the end of Systems Planning, the area believes a major investment is warranted in one or more corridors, it identifies a priority corridor and requests UMTA's permission to begin an Alternatives Analysis.

Alternatives Analysis includes a more detailed examination of the potential ridership and estimates the costs of a number of options in the selected corridor, including the UMTA-required Transportation Systems Management (TSM) option. This involves low capital cost improvements such as upgrading the bus service, priority lanes and other service enhancement techniques. At the end of the Alternatives Analysis, the local agency notifies UMTA of its preferred alternative and requests permission to begin the Preliminary Engineering Design. Usually they request discretionary Federal funds to do the Preliminary Engineering Design as this can cost several million dollars.

Permission to advance to Preliminary Engineering Design is granted if the project appears to be cost-effective and adequate funding is available, locally and federally, to assure its completion and operation. However, Congress has mandated that UMTA advance certain projects into Preliminary Engineering Design in spite of UMTA's reservations under these criteria. Preliminary Engineering Design is followed by Final Design and actual construction.

UMTA has developed criteria for examining the cost effectiveness of proposed projects, based on the cost of attracting a new transit rider. There are two indices - the Federal index and the Total index. The indices are computed as shown in Table 3.

TABLE 3
COMPUTATION OF INDICES FOR US RAPID TRANSIT ASSESSMENT

$$\text{Federal index} = \frac{D(ACP) + D(AOC) - D(ATT) - D(ALF)}{D(ARIDERS)}$$

$$\text{Total index} = \frac{D(ACP) + D(AOC) - D(ATT)}{D(ARIDERS)}$$

Where ACP is the annualised total capital cost
AOC is the annual operating cost
ATT are the travel time savings
ALF is the annualised local capital funding
ARIDERS is the number of annual transit journeys
and D( ) is the change compared to the TSM alternative.

Both indices measure the average cost for an additional journey. The Federal index considers the cost in terms of federal money only, while the total index includes all costs.

To enter the Alternatives Analysis, a corridor must satisfy two tests. It must have a current daily total of more than 15,000 public transport journeys. It must also achieve an index (cost per additional transit rider net of time savings) within an upper limit of $10 per additional rider, based on generous estimates of the operating cost, parking cost and travel time savings.

In order to pass from Alternatives Analysis to Preliminary Engineering, projects must satisfy three criteria. The project must produce a gain in ridership compared with the TSM alternative. The alternative must lie on the so-called cost effective frontier, which means that there is no other option which would produce more additional riders for less money. The project must also at this stage achieve an index within an upper limit of $6 per additional transit rider.

Once projects pass to the Preliminary Design, they are almost certain to receive funding for the full system.

UMTA originally provided grants of eighty per cent of the total cost. When systems overran their budget, UMTA was often asked for further funds. This is now dealt with by UMTA stipulating that any overrun in spend must be paid for locally. There has been consideration given to adjusting the level of grant according to the amount of private money involved. Obviously, more systems could be supported if the money was spread more thinly. There has been a recent tendency for grants to be awarded at less than the eighty per cent.

4.2   Washington, DC

4.2.1   The urban area

The Washington Metropolitan Area Transit Authority (WMATA) was established in 1967 through a congressionally approved interstate compact to provide public transportation in the national capital region. The transit area includes parts of the states of Maryland and Virginia as well as Washington D.C. The eight Washington area jurisdictions served by WMATA cover 1,489 square miles and have a population of 2.9 million people.

The Metro system is the product of more than 50 years of discussion and nearly three decades of congressional and citizen efforts. It was built to provide an alternative to the construction of the planned radial freeway system into and through the Downtown.

An initial 25 mile system costing $150 million was approved by Congress in 1965. Work actually started in 1969. In December of the same year Congress passed legislation authorising federal participation in a 97.7 mile Metro system to the extent of $1.1 billion over ten years (approximately £720 million at current rates of exchange). Congress has continued to support the development of the system through legislation. The system when complete will now be 103 miles in length.

4.2.2   Development of the system

Metro was designed to be aesthetically compatible with the history and symbolism of the nation's capital. Most of the stations are underground. They are all of a similar design within huge spacious vaults. Platforms, mezzanines, escalators and lifts were built freestanding within the vaults, putting walls beyond the reach of vandals. Materials were selected to be durable and to give a sense of timelessness, for example, concrete, brick and granite. Individual stations currently cost up to $40 million.

There are four Metro lines, as shown in Figure 4.1. The first section to open was a 4.2 mile length of the Red line with five stations. The service was initially from 6 a.m. to 8 p.m. on weekdays only. The Blue line opened one year later, linking central Washington with National Airport. This brought the system up to 17.6 miles and 25 stations. In 1978, the Orange line opened out to New Carrollton and the Red line was extended to Silver Spring. Extensions have been added steadily to bring the current system to 70 miles of line and 64 stations. There are about 600 operating rail cars.

As the system developed geographically, the times of operation were also extended. In 1978, the weekday operation was extended from 8 p.m. to midnight and a Saturday service was introduced with the same hours of operation. A daytime Sunday service came into operation during 1979 and this was extended to midnight in 1986.

As well as operating the Metrorail, WMATA operate 1,562 buses on 344 bus routes. There are approximately 8,000 employees.

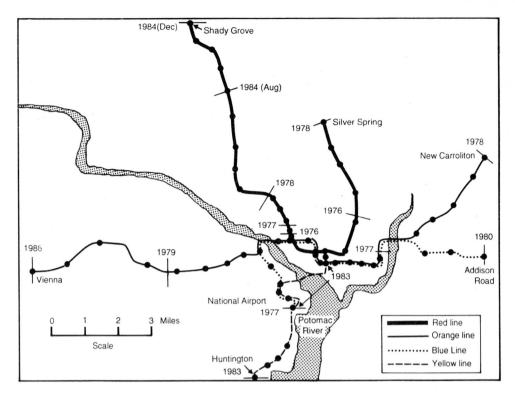

Fig 4.1   Washington Metro

4.2.3   Capital costs

Financing for Metrorail is complex because it involves the federal government, two state governments and eight political jurisdictions. Metrorail construction is funded with federal and local money, currently provided on a 80/20 percent federal/local basis. The method of raising the local money varies throughout the eight authorities. In Maryland State, there is a gasoline tax of 2 cents per gallon for mass transit investment. In Virginia, there is a 1 per cent tax on gasoline, but the state government makes an additional contribution from general funds. In Washington, there are various sources.

The system to date has cost $5.01 billion (approximately £3,200 million at current rates), including a transfer of $2.16 billion from the inter-state highway fund. By legislation passed in 1974, the highway authority could transfer money from highway schemes to mass transit investment. Spending has been at a rate of about $250 million per annum (£160 million) for each of the past four years.

WMATA has financing for a further 19.5 miles. The Red and Yellow lines are being extended and a new Green line is being built to serve the South-East and North-East sectors of the metropolitan area. Additional funding will be required to complete the remaining nine stations and 13.5 miles of the full 103 mile system. This funding is now being sought through Congress.

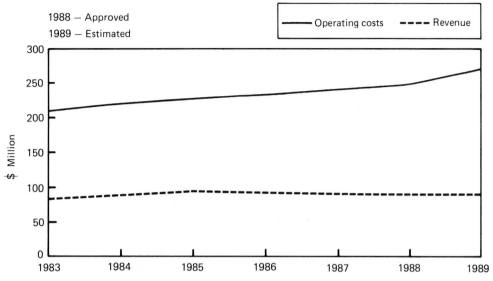

Fig 4.2   *Washington Bus - Operating costs and revenue*

4.2.4   Operating costs

The Washington Transit system recovers 53 per cent of operating costs through revenue, advertising, bus charter and contract services. The Metrorail system covers 74 per cent of operating costs compared to 34 per cent for the bus system. The remaining 47 per cent of operating costs is financed mostly through local sources, although there is a small (3 per cent) federal subsidy. Figures 4.2 and 4.3 show how bus and rail costs compare with revenue since 1982. The cost allocation formulae to distribute the net costs between the eight jurisdictions are quite complex.

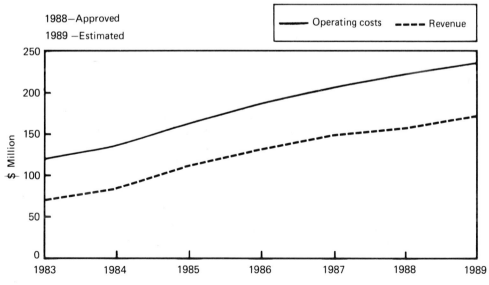

Fig 4.3   *Washington Metro - Operating costs and revenue*

4.2.5 Patronage

The annual ridership on the WMATA system is currently 144 million passengers on train and 140 million passengers on bus. This amounts to a total of 243 million journeys per year, of which 17 per cent are interchange journeys (see Figure 4.4). Patronage has increased by 35 per cent since 1982, due almost entirely to more journeys being made on the expanding Metrorail system. Fifteen per cent of residents in the WMATA area use Metro in an average weekday. Figures 4.5 and 4.6 show how the passenger increases are related to service levels.

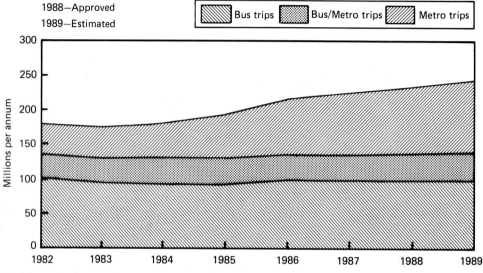

Fig 4.4   Washington - Bus and Metro ridership

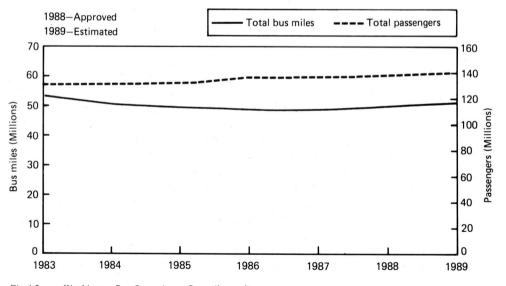

Fig 4.5   Washington Bus Operations - Bus miles and passengers

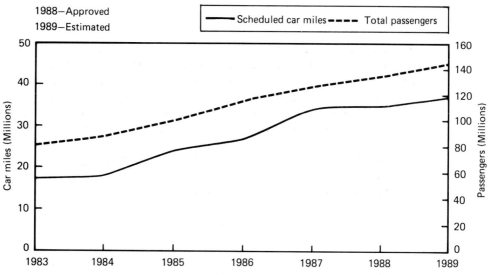

——— Scheduled car miles ▪▪▪▪ Total passengers

Fig 4.6   Washington Metro Operations - Car miles and passengers

4.2.6   Land use development

Washington is a national capital city and as such is very sensitive to the general economic climate within the United States. For example, spending on goods and services in the Washington area increased from $6 billion to $13 billion in the last five years. With the concentration of federal employment within the capital, government policies can have a major influence on the number and location of jobs. The construction and rapid development of the Washington Beltway, and consequential developments such as Tysons' Corner (75,000 jobs, 3 million square feet of shopping space, 8 department stores) have had a dramatic effect on the city and confuse any consideration of the effect of the Metrorail alone. The Metrorail system has been steadily extended so that it now provides a service to almost all of the downtown Washington area and therefore provides little in the way of control areas with which to compare the effects.

Washington has a buoyant and expanding economy. There is a strong demand for office and retail space and this is most obviously being accommodated around the suburban fringe. Scope for development in the heart of the city is limited. However, new centres are emerging. Alexandria and Silver Spring are examples of rapid new development around Metrorail stations.

Alexandria is a largely residential city about 5 miles south of Washington that has placed a high priority on restoring its 18th century houses and enhancing its waterfront. In 1981 the city had 4.2 million square feet of office space. The Metroline was extended to Alexandria in 1983 and the three new stations provided connections to Washington city and to National Airport. The Washington Beltway also provides access to the southern part of Alexandria with beltway developments growing up around Eisenhower Station. In 1987, city planners reported plans for a further 10 million square feet of commercial office space, bringing the total to 19 million square feet if all the plans were realised. Construction of these offices is evident now, with the area around King Street Station now being almost totally redeveloped.

Paradoxically, while the new development seems to have been attracted to the city by the significant improvements in transportation, both private and public, few employees of such offices use the Metro. Of 724 employees surveyed, only 6 per cent rode Metrobus or Metrorail and this is causing considerable problems for local traffic management. This concern gave rise to suggestions that the city would place restrictions on the number of car parking spaces allowed and this may in turn have created a surge in plan submissions. Some of the developments are still under construction and may well attract new staff to public transport when they are complete.

As one travels out along the Red line to Silver Spring station, the land use densities fall rapidly and the line runs on an existing rail track behind the development which lies alongside a main suburban highway. There are few development possibilities along this part of the line as the stations are quite far apart and there is excellent access by car. However at the end of the line, Silver Spring station is surrounded by tall new office blocks. When the station opened in 1978, Maryland State Government spent substantial funds in improving the roads and environment, expecting a surge in development. This was slow to develop, but in 1980 the first building adjacent to the station created a market and land prices have risen dramatically as the other developments have followed.

4.2.7   WMATA initiatives

By federal law, WMATA may only use land for transportation purposes. Any land surplus to requirements must be sold at market rates with a return of 80 per cent to federal authorities. This limits WMATA in promoting development through the joint development programme.

The WMATA joint development programme has three aspects. The first aspect is joint development involving long term leases for air rights. This has been quite successful and at present is generating $4 million per year. The second aspect is the provision of system interfaces. This is where special access to Metro stations is provided to adjacent developments and developers pay a contribution ranging from $10,000 to $1 million for a 10 to 30 year lease. The third aspect is where WMATA attempt to encourage symbiotic development around Metro stations without any direct financial involvement from the developer.

The Silver Spring development at the end of the Red line is an example of a system interface. It had been hoped that there would be a joint development at the station, but this has been delayed for another few years. The area is being developed rapidly, but not quite in the way hoped by WMATA.

Local authorities attempt to assist Metro by appropriate land use zoning. However, this is difficult to sustain and, despite the application of maximum floor area ratios in areas not served by Metrorail, developers still manage to build larger developments than permitted by the zoning. In Maryland, Public Facilities Agreements have been applied whereby development is restricted to areas where there are adequate public facilities, such as roads and public transport.

4.2.8   Employment

A study was conducted by the Metropolitan Washington Council of Governments (COG) into the changes in employment over the period 1980-85. The Metrorail impact area was defined as 7/10 mile or fifteen minutes walk from any Metro station.

It was found that over the five year period, while total employment had increased by 15 per cent, employment in the Metrorail station areas had increased by 7 per cent. This compares with an increase of 26 per cent in the areas outside Metrorail. The majority of jobs (52 per cent) were still located in the Metro station areas, but the proportion declined by four per cent between 1980 and 1985.

With the exception of state and local government, each employment sector in the economy experienced a higher change in employment in areas outside the Metrorail areas compared with inside. Federal government employment, which decreased overall, showed a large decrease in Metrorail areas and a small increase elsewhere.

This study highlights the difficulty of isolating the effects of the Metrorail investment from other demographic changes. Many large cities are experiencing a migration of employment from the city centre to the suburbs and the Washington Beltway has certainly encouraged this in Washington. It would seem that the attraction of new development to the areas near Metrorail is counterbalanced by a trend for greater dispersal of jobs.

4.2.9 Overall Conclusions about the Effect of Metrorail Investment.

A report written for the West Midlands Passenger Transport Executive in England (Linford 1988) contains details of a number of land use and development changes in Washington and claims these as positive effects of the Metro. However, views are divided on whether the changes were definitely caused by the Metrorail investment, and the view of the Federal authorities is much less enthusiastic.

With regard to new developments, WMPTE report that Metro station areas, which amount to two per cent of the region, captured 43 per cent of the region's commercial development between 1980 and 1986. Similarly, the City Council claimed that Metro had played a major role in $970 million worth of buildings, completed or under construction near Metro stations. However, it is difficult to judge whether the figure of 43 per cent is more than would have been expected without the Metro. American cities traditionally have a small, very tightly defined central business district within which most of the prestigious development takes place. In Washington, most of the signs of new development are in the CBD, with less evidence as one moves further out from the centre. As the Metro serves practically all the CBD, one would *expect* a large proportion of new development near the Metro.

On the other hand, there is currently an even greater boom in development in the outskirts of Washington, as can be seen by the rapid development along the beltway, most of which is not served by Metro. The value of this development is probably much greater than that of development near the Metro. It is also significant to note that during the same period, employment around stations increased at a *slower* rate than elsewhere. The real test of the effect of the Metro would be seen in a recession, not in conditions of economic expansion.

WMPTE also reported that new stations had rejuvenated fading shopping districts. Metro had transformed third-class locations into heavily sought after first-class property.

Examination of housing sales along the Metro route showed that homes near stations appreciated at a faster rate than similar homes further away. The rate of increase was greatest in areas that had potential for improvement or gentrification anyway, or in areas close to downtown Washington, though the increase in prices was believed to have occurred at all stations.

In summary, there were signs that the Washington Metrorail system attracted some of the demand for development and improved the value of properties along the line. These effects should be viewed alongside the fact that the Metro cost $5,000 million and is one of the finest systems in the world in one of the finest capitals. It is unlikely that many other systems could be more attractive to developers.

4.3   Baltimore, Maryland

4.3.1   The urban area

Baltimore is an industrial city. However, many of the major industries have been in decline and there has been rapid growth on the periphery of city as people move out of the city centre to lower density housing. Offices, shopping centres and new industrial complexes are being developed on the periphery of the urban area to serve the new housing. Consequently, the population of Baltimore has declined drastically in the last few years. Six years ago Baltimore had a population of 1 million which has now fallen to 650,000 people. The city has received a great deal of federal aid for urban development and this is particularly evident around the harbour area which has been completely redeveloped and is now a very attractive area with restaurants, sailing ships and new office blocks.

4.3.2   Organisation of public transport

The public transport system in Baltimore is a function of the state government. There are seven modal agencies - Highways, the Airport, Car registration, Toll facilities, the State railroad, Port Administration and the Mass Transit Administration. These agencies collect revenues and fees which are paid into a central fund. This is then redistributed according to need. Revenue from the Maryland State fuel tax is also paid into the fund. There is considerable flexibility in funding transportation investment as the state allocates money for all forms of transportation investment and the MTA is directly answerable to the Governor of Maryland. The ex-mayor of Baltimore is now the Governor of the State and has supported the investments in the heavy rail line and the new tramway.

MTA operates 900 buses directly and also contracts 8 or 9 lines in remote areas where it does not operate directly. There are 2,800 employees. The average age of the bus fleet is six years. In 1983, the average age of the bus fleet was 11 years. MTA then began a fleet replacement policy of eighty buses per year and they are now in the seventh year of this programme.

4.3.3   Development of the heavy metro system

Baltimore had an electric tram car system, the last one of which ran in 1963. The current bus lines reflect the routes of the original street cars. The reason for the loss of street cars was the growing car ownership which led to the loss of passengers and the increased congestion brought about by these cars which reduced the reliability of the street cars with a further loss of passengers. The plan for investment in rail was developed in the sixties soon after the demise of the tramways. The master plan involved six radial lines from the centre of Baltimore. However, the decision to go ahead with the first line was only narrowly passed as Baltimore came at the end of the vogue for heavy rail system investment.

Construction of the first line, Section A, began in 1976 and the line was opened in 1983. This consists of an 8 mile stretch from the city centre to Reisterstown Plaza. Four miles of the system is in tunnel with 4 miles on elevated track. The line was extended by 6 miles to Owings Mills in 1987 (Figure 4.7).

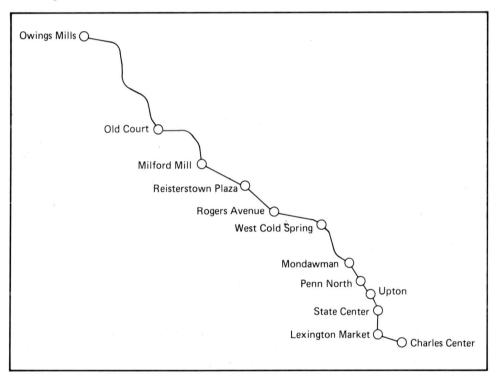

Fig 4.7   Baltimore Metro

4.3.4   The extension to John Hopkins Hospital

Approval was received in 1985 to build a one and a half mile extension to John Hopkins Hospital. The hospital employs 15,000 people, many of whom are lower grade staff who use transit and come from the northwest of the city, along the current rail line. There are two stations on the extension, one of these stations is under conduits carrying the John Falls river. The deepest station

59

on the system is 120 feet down. The line will cost between $300 million and $320 million to build. The money is coming from an interstate highway funds transfer.

4.3.5 The new tramway

In 1987 the Mass Transit Administration began a feasibility study to decide what to do about further extensions. This was based on cheaper solutions than the high cost heavy rail existing system. Operating costs are a problem with the heavy rail system. For example, the system is not operated on a Sunday as staff are needed at every station. Four lines were investigated for the new tramway and a line running south from the city centre was selected as the best option. However, following political consultation it was decided to go for a line from the north of the city through the centre to the south of the city. This was proposed in December 1987 and the construction work began in June 1989, with a view to completing the system by November 1991.

The feasibility study for the tramway looked at four aspects: technical feasibility, capital and operating costs, environmental effects and ridership. The study took 6-8 months. It was not an attempt to develop a master plan for rail, but rather an immediate solution to the next stage of development. The southern portion was selected on cost grounds. The west line had the greatest ridership but also greater costs.

The planned tramway (Figure 4.8) is 22 miles in length and will have stations on average every three quarters of a mile. There will be 1,000 car parking spaces at each end, the maximum speed of the tram will be 55 mph but the normal speed will be 35 mph. It will actually be slower to travel by tram from the distant terminus to the city centre than by car, but the problems of congestion are thought to make the tram an attractive alternative. At the moment buses run along the highway which runs parallel to the tramway, but there are considerable difficulties in running the services at unsocial hours and the tramway will enable them to be reduced. The new tramway starts at the airport in the south, runs through the centre of the business district, along a street which contains very poor quality shops and is in great need of redevelopment, then out along the route of an expressway to the north of the city. The southern part of the expressway runs through a wooded valley and there is very little opportunity for development but further out there are a number of possibilities.

4.3.6 Fares

The fare system for both the Metro and bus network are based on a zonal system, with four radial zones. Charges are 90 cents for a journey in 1 zone up to 1.45 for a journey for 4 zones. A bus transfer can be added for an additional 10 cents. It is also possible to buy tickets in packs of 10 and to get a monthly pass for unlimited travel.

4.3.7 Costs and funding

The state has directed MTA to recover 50 per cent of direct operating costs through revenue. For capital investment in public transport, the state has directed that two thirds must come from federal funds. However, this ruling was recently modified to require only 10 per cent from federal funds for rapid transit investment. The latest extension to the line has been planned on that basis.

60

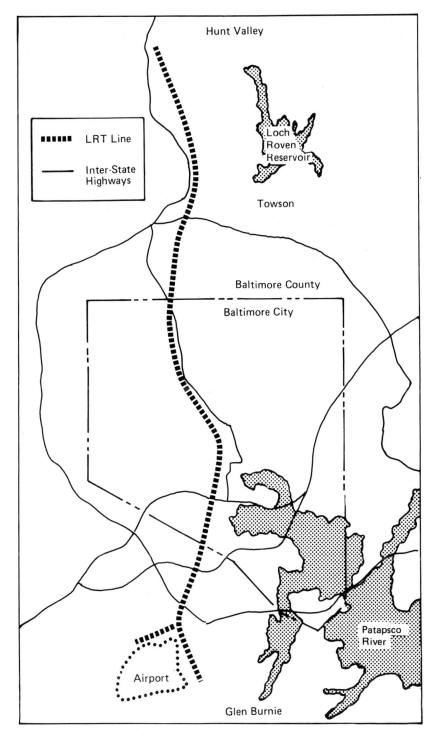

Legend:
- ▪▪▪▪▪▪ LRT Line
- —— Inter-State Highways

Hunt Valley

Loch
Roven
Reservoir

Towson

Baltimore County

Baltimore City

Airport

Patapsco
River

Glen Burnie

Fig 4.8   Baltimore Central LRT: Proposed Tramway

For the first line, Section A, the estimated cost was $750 million and the actual cost was $790 million. Funding came mostly from federal sources. The line was extended by 6 miles between 1984 and 1987 by the addition of section B. This required a transfer of funds from the highway programme to pay for 85 per cent of the cost. For section B the estimated cost was $180 million and the actual cost was $140 million. In 1985 there was a further transfer of $320 million to enable the one and a half mile extension to the hospital to be built.

It was decided to use State funds for the majority of the $290 million for the new tramway. $205 million is to come from the State Transportation Trust Fund. The City of Baltimore and the two surrounding counties will provide $15 million each and this is already committed. The additional $40 million is being sought through federal funds as the MTA have a requirement to raise 10 per cent of the funds through federal sources. The overall project proposal has not needed to follow the UMTA guidelines but they will be followed for the $40 million funding. The part of the line which is being submitted for federal funding is the extension to the main Amtrak Station, the airport and the northern section of the line.

4.3.8   Patronage

The overall bus and train system carries 300,000 trips per day, or 82 million per year. The estimated daily ridership for line A was 83,000, the actual ridership was 45,000. On Sections A and B together the estimated ridership was 110,000, the actual ridership is 53,000 so Baltimore MTA have estimated costs reasonably well and overestimated passengers by a factor of 2. The estimated additional passengers for the one and a half mile extension for section C was 30,000 and may be optimistic. The estimate of 35,000 passengers for the tramway is thought to be more realistic, in the light of experience.

Travel patterns are changing. In the past, most morning travel focused on the centre of the city. Now, with the proliferation and expansion of large suburban employment centres, traffic is significant both towards and away from the downtown area.

4.3.9   Development effects

There are very few signs of the Metro having influenced land use or development at this fairly early stage. As has already been stated, the city has been losing population and going through a transformation from manufacturing to service industries. Federal assistance has been influential in this change, but has been concentrated in the centre of the city.

The land use density falls rapidly as one travels out along the rail line and much of the new line runs along a previous heavy rail track. The development is usually set well back from the line and often fronts onto parallel highways, with consequential good access by car and with plenty of parking.

The Owings Mills area at the end of the line was planned as a new suburban centre where development would be concentrated to protect the countryside elsewhere. However, the station area is dominated by a huge park-and-ride site with spaces for 3,500 cars and occupying 35 acres. Next to this is a large shopping mall in 30 acres of car parking space. This massive provision for cars has rather reduced the opportunities to develop the station area further, although it would be possible to build over the car park.

Along the downtown part of the heavy rail line there is residential development of poor quality and few options for any new development. The city centre has received a considerable boost from the injection of federal funding to revitalise the area. At Charles Centre, the end of the line, the Mass Transit Authority have leased a site for a 30 storey bank headquarters and the MTA receive $500,000 in rent each year from this development. The MTA has very limited powers for development, being limited to developing sites for transportation purposes.

MTA is an arm of the State Government and so has no direct involvement in land use decisions. The outcome is that land-use policies are not always well coordinated with transport decisions. In particular Baltimore City is continuing to provide more parking space and is therefore not pursuing policies to support transit. The city does not suffer severe traffic congestion.

4.4   Atlanta, Georgia

4.4.1   The urban area

Metropolitan Atlanta is a seven county region consisting of 1.8 million people. Atlanta, with a population of 425,000, is the largest of more than 50 cities within the region.

Atlanta's significant growth and prosperity can be linked very closely to the development of transportation. Atlanta was born at the junction of three railroads in 1836. Radial highways were then constructed to reach the railhead at Atlanta from all directions. The city began to grow outwards along these highway corridors. In the 1880s, streetcars were introduced and were very heavily used. This helped to consolidate the central business district. The arrival of buses in 1914 enabled the areas between the major highways to be developed. The growth in private cars completed the process. New freeways followed and encouraged the spreading of the urban area as far as 30 miles from the centre. Suburban shopping centres and industrial parks sprang up on the outskirts of the urban area, drawing people away from the CBD. Recent heavy investment in freeway improvement has encouraged further traffic growth.

The emergence of Atlanta as a regional and national airline centre has also assisted the growth of the area. Atlanta airport is the busiest in the world, being designed to handle 55 million passengers per year. The Automated Guideway Transit (AGT) system, which connects the ticketing and baggage areas to the concourses is the fifth busiest transit system in the world, carrying more passengers than the BART system in San Francisco. It is just over one mile in length.

It is perhaps not surprising therefore, that the development of the rapid transit was considered from the start as an instrument of urban planning.

4.4.2 Operation of public transport

The Metropolitan Atlanta Rapid Transit Authority (MARTA) was created by an act of the Georgia legislature in 1965 for the purpose of building and operating a comprehensive bus/rapid transit system to serve the needs of the Atlanta Metropolitan Area. The counties of Clayton, DeKalb, Fulton and Gwinnett are represented on the Board of Directors. In 1971, DeKalb and Fulton Counties approved a one-per cent sales tax, the first of its kind in the USA, to finance the local share of the capital investments and operation of the rail and bus system.

Bus and rail services are fully integrated. This is illustrated by the fact that about 40 per cent of Metro passengers arrive or depart at the station by bus.

4.4.3 Development of the system

The development of plans for a rapid transit system in Metropolitan Atlanta was historically unique in that the system was initially conceived and planned by a comprehensive planning agency. The five county Atlanta Regional Metropolitan Planning Commission (ARMPC) evaluated various rail options and published the rapid transit component of the Atlanta Regional Comprehensive Plan in 1961.

The Transit Station Area Development Studies (TSADS) were conceived and designed by the Atlanta Regional Commission(ARC) within a tripartite agreement between ARC, MARTA and the Georgia Department of Transportation (GDOT). The studies had two main purposes:-

-       To plan for the development, redevelopment, or conservation of areas surrounding stations, thereby maximising the developmental opportunities of the rapid transit system.

-       To protect established communities by designing mechanisms to minimise disruption which could occur as a result of system construction.

All planning agencies were involved - local governments, ARC, MARTA, GDOT. The programme was federally funded. TSADS formally came to an end in 1975, but it marked the beginning of a process of control and management of development which has continued through the life of the system. Local officials became aware of the potential for development and positively encouraged it by channelling funds into station area improvements and by introducing new zoning ordinances.

The creation of MARTA Special Public Interest Districts (MSPI) were part of the policy designed to promote growth and mixed development in station areas.

The lines were established to meet two land use needs. These were:-

a.   The need to serve existing concentrations of residential, commercial, and industrial development, and

b.   The need to intensify future land use development in appropriate locations along the MARTA line.

64

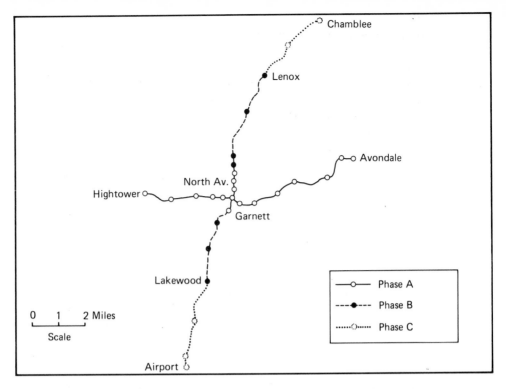

Fig 4.9   Atlanta Metro

Plans to reconstruct the areas around stations have been an integral part of the overall planning process. The full system was planned as a 53 mile network served by 39 stations and supplemented by 8 miles of busways with 2 stations. This included 16 miles of elevated line, 10 of subway and 27 miles at grade. The first part of the line, the East/West line from Avondale to Hightower, opened in June and December of 1979. Short sections were added to the North and South lines in 1982. Further sections were added in 1984 and 1986, when the line reached Atlanta airport.

At present, the North/South line is 20.3 miles in length with 17 stations. The East/West line is 11.8 miles with 13 stations (Figure 4.9).

MARTA is currently at work on the final designs for extensions to Doraville, Kensington and Indian Creek Stations. Doraville, a two mile extension beyond Chamblee on the Northern line, is expected to open in December 1992. Kensington and Indian Creek will extend the East line 3.1 miles beyond Avondale and are expected to open in June 1993.

A planned branch line off the Northern line has now been changed from a busway to a rail line. The line will run down the central island of a new highway which is yet to be built. The extension will be funded locally as the federal funding process takes a long time.

A short spur of 1.5 miles on the West line to Bankhead is being funded locally and will cost about $50 million. It is expected to open in 1992.

65

As well as investing in the rail system, MARTA has also upgraded the bus network. Over 500 new buses were added to the fleet, new shelters were installed and the bus fare was reduced to 15 cents. Service levels were increased from 19 million bus miles to 30 million bus miles in 1978. The 1989 service levels are the same, although fares have been increased substantially.

4.4.4   Service levels

On weekdays the system runs on a regular six minute headway from 6 a.m. until 8 p.m. and then at a ten minute headway until 1.00 a.m. On Saturdays, the system runs on a constant ten minute headway and on Sundays the headway is fifteen minutes. Some trains stop short so headways at the ends of the line are longer.

4.4.5   Costs and funding

The rapid transit system has cost $2.5 billion to date (£1650 million at current rates). Federal funding amounts to 57 per cent, local funding to 43 per cent. Federal grants of 80 per cent have been awarded for parts of the system. Local funding has mainly been raised by means of the sales tax.

The operating cost of the rapid transit is $179.6 million. The state law requires MARTA to recover 35 per cent of the previous year's costs in revenue. Over the last few years, the federal contribution to operating subsidy has been reduced and there is a 50 per cent limit on the use of the sales tax revenue for operating subsidy. Consequently, fares have had to rise from 50 cents flat fare in 1980 to 85 cents now.

4.4.6   Patronage

The rapid transit system currently carries 196,000 passengers on an average weekday, compared with 289,000 passengers making bus trips. There are a large number of transfer trips, both between bus and rail and between the North/South and East/West rail lines.

4.4.7   Effects on urban development

MARTA stations were classified into five types. These were:-

a.   High intensity urban node
b.   Regional mixed-use node
c.   Commuter transit node
d.   Neighbourhood mixed-use node
e.   Neighbourhood residential node

Each station area was divided into concentric zones - an inner impact zone, a transition zone and a preservation zone. Station Area Advisory Committees were established for every station plan and the city council prepared a strategy of implementation following consultation with local residents. These strategies included changes in zoning categories, parking regulations, air rights development, provision of pedestrian access and provision of new facilities such as schools and landscaping. Some of these objectives were to be achieved with public funds and others by private investment.

The plan was to enable the city, the developers and MARTA to work together to achieve the intended changes. Developers have had confidence in the process and have responded. Large land holdings have been acquired and there are numerous examples of large prestigious developments, particularly along the northern line.

The rate of development varies very much in line with the plans set out in the early Station Area studies. Development along the East/West line was intended to be minimal and there are few signs of recent change. There were attempts at a few developments, but these have so far been unsuccessful. This line serves mostly the poorer residential and industrial areas of the city and so is less likely to attract profitable development. At Decatur, the last but one station at the Eastern end of the line, there were plans for considerable development, but these have so far been difficult to achieve.

The Southern line passes through a similar, though more industrial, area than that along the East/West line, and then out to the Airport. Attempts to encourage new development in this rather run-down part of the city have not produced much response. It will require a great deal of 'encouragement' to draw developers to these areas.

In contrast to the other three sections of the line, development is occurring all the way along the Northern line. The stations nearer to the city centre are those identified for intense development and the rate of change now being experienced is enormous. High rise offices, hotels and apartments have been built at these stations and the pressure for continued development is moving out along the line. There are plans for a large business park near Brookhaven which may include a people mover to bring people to the rapid transit station. Such is the demand for and profitability of development in the area. Office blocks are being interfaced with stations through joint development.

MARTA has the same restrictions as other public transport operators which preclude involvement in joint development. However, good use has been made of surplus land and of air rights exploitation. Of course, MARTA is strongly supported by the policies and decisions of the planning authorities and by the Mayor of Atlanta who has been instrumental in attracting businesses to the city. Federal money was also involved in the early days to produce the plans and to assist the evolution of the planning process to implement them.

Atlanta has had the advantage of growth. By establishing a strong planning process which include good incentives, the planning authorities have been very successful in channelling that growth. However, there are limits to where developers will invest and some of the poorer areas have not yet attracted development. As has been seen elsewhere, the rail system serves to speed up the rate of development in growth areas, but does less to assist declining areas.

4.5 San Diego, California

4.5.1 The urban area

San Diego County lies at the southern end of California and covers 4,200 square miles. The urbanised area is mainly contained within the coastal plain and foothills. The eastern two thirds of the county consists of mountains and desert. San Diego is relatively isolated from the rest of California with mountains to the east, the Pacific Ocean to the West and a large area of military land to the north. The southern boundary is on the Mexican border. The population of the county is about 2 million. The population in San Diego has grown from about 100,000 in the 1940s to about 1 million now. Between 1970 and 1980, the San Diego region's population grew by 37 per cent.

The city was dominated by military and aerospace activities through to the early 1960's. The naval presence is still very strong, accounting for 100,000 jobs in direct employment and twice that number in associated employment. The city has Mexican quarters and immigrant quarters, with a great deal of small scale, poor quality housing developed on the hillsides surrounding the central city. The downtown area is booming with new development and attractive facilities around the harbour.

Despite the eight 10-lane freeways there is quite a lot of congestion, especially on the I-5 to the north, the 163 to the northeast and on the J-8 east-west. Parking costs are up to $110 per month in core.

4.5.2 The public transport system

The San Diego Metropolitan Transit Development Board (MTDB) was created by state law in 1975, with the specific charge to plan and implement a fixed guideway system. There is one light rail operator, five fixed route bus operators, five taxi-based dial-a-ride services and four accessible dial-a-ride services. In addition, private jitneys primarily serve the military areas. San Diego Trolley Inc (SDTI) is organised as a public corporation which runs the trolley, and San Diego Transit Corporation runs the bus service between the local communities. Both are subsidiaries of MTDB , which owns their assets. Three of the other bus services are municipal operations which run through contracts with private operators; the fourth bus service is a private line operating for profit without subsidy.

4.5.3 Development of the Trolley

4.5.3.1 The south line

The San Diego Trolley (Figure 4.10) is a light rail system, using manually operated Siemens-Duwag U2 trams on an exclusive right of way with minimal grade separation. The first line of the Trolley opened in the summer of 1981 and was the first modern light rail system in the USA. It is 15.9 miles in length and operates between the city centre and the Mexican border at San Ysidro. It operates along existing streets for 1.7 miles in the city centre and has six stops. For the

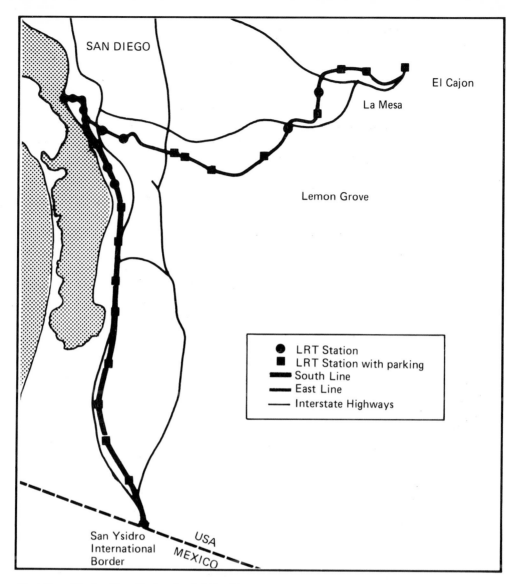

Fig 4.10   The San Diego Trolley: South & East Line

next 14 miles, the trolley uses rehabilitated main-line track taken over from the San Diego and Arizona Eastern (SD & AE) railway. A freeway runs parallel to the rail line for much of its length and there are numerous level crossings between the trolley and the freeway access roads. At the southern terminus the trolley once more uses a public street for a short distance to the international border crossing with Mexico.

There are twelve stations on this part of the line. All have simple, low-level platforms with a shelter, bench, transit information and public telephone. Local bus routes have been modified to serve the Trolley.

4.5.3.2 The east line

The East Line follows the same track as the South Line through the city centre and then turns east at Imperial and 12th Station. Four stations and 4.5 miles of line as far as Euclid Avenue station opened in 1986. An extra 11.1 miles with eight stations extended the line to El Cajon in June 1989.

The final 3.33 mile section of the east line will have four stations and terminate in Santee town centre. Preliminary Engineering for this part of the line is in progress.

4.5.3.3 Other extensions to the system

The Bayside Line is a 2.0 mile section which will link the current two ends of the line through the city centre to form a loop around the central area. This will involve 5 new stations and improving an existing station through a joint development project. The projected cost is $40 million and the line is expected to open in 1990.

There are various other extensions in different stages of planning to bring the ultimate system to 112.6 miles in length.

4.5.4   Service levels

On weekdays the service runs at 15 minute headways from 5 am until 8 pm (10 pm on South Line), then half hourly until 1 am. At weekends the early morning headways are half hourly. The trams run at an average speed of 9 mph through the city centre and 30 mph elsewhere.

4.5.5   Costs and funding

The first line cost $117.6 million. Nearly 90 per cent of the funding came from California state petrol tax revenues and the remainder came from state sales tax revenues. Of the 7.5 per cent sales tax, 0.5 per cent is allocated for investment. One third of this is for transit and 80 per cent of that is for capital investment in rapid transit.

The first part of the East Line to Euclid Avenue cost $33.6 million and was also funded locally. State petrol tax provided 75 per cent, sale and leaseback arrangements 12 per cent. The remainder came from State transportation funds. The extension of the second line to El Cajon was federally funded from the UMTA discretionary programme. The total cost was $108 million, $58.3 million (54 per cent) federal grant, $39.5 million (36 per cent) state petrol and sales tax and $10.2 million (10 per cent) from local transportation funds. The new sections of line involve some requests for federal assistance.

Revenues cover more than 90 per cent of the operating costs for the trolley. For bus and rail combined the percentage covered is just less than 50 per cent. About a third of all public transport journeys in the San Diego area involve the trolley.

The State Transportation Development Act (TDA) monies provide approximately 40 per cent of the total transit operating funds in the MTDB area. The TDA account is funded by revenue from one quarter of one per cent state sales tax. This is apportioned on the basis of population.

4.5.6 Patronage

In 1989, there were 8.3 million person trips in the region each day. Of these 1.2 million, or 14.5 per cent occurred in the trolley corridor. The public transport modal share within the corridor just before the trolley opened was 3.6 per cent, twice the average for the region.

The initial estimate for trolley patronage on the first line was 10,000 passengers per day. Patronage throughout 1982 and 1983 was around 11,000 passengers per day and this rose to between 14,000 and 15,000 per day when the headways were reduced to 15 minutes. Overall transit use increased by 20 per cent in the three years after the first trolley line opened (Figure 4.11).

The trolley is heavily used by tourists and Mexican residents, so weekend and summer travel is relatively high. Saturday ridership is about 10 per cent less than weekday use, with Sunday patronage being only about 25 per cent less than weekdays.

The average trip length on the trolley is over 8 miles, showing that the system is used more as a suburban railway. Twenty per cent of the trip ends are at the Mexican border which accommodates a total of 52,000 people per day crossing into the United States.

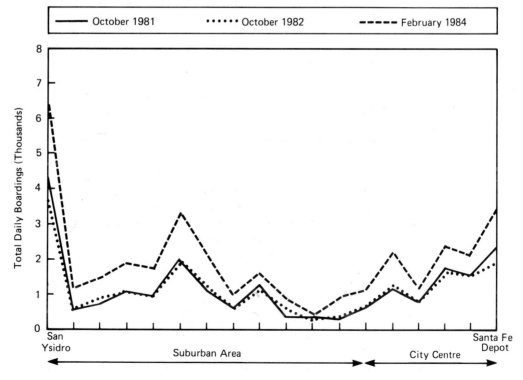

Fig 4.11   San Diego Trolley - South Line patronage

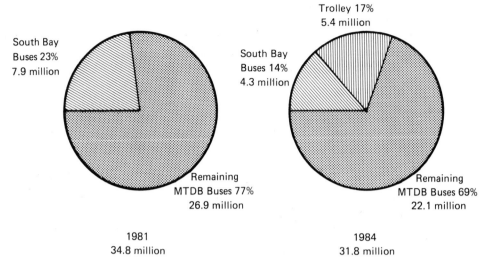

South Bay
Buses 23%
7.9 million

Trolley 17%
5.4 million

South Bay
Buses 14%
4.3 million

Remaining
MTDB Buses 77%
26.9 million

Remaining
MTDB Buses 69%
22.1 million

1981
34.8 million

1984
31.8 million

Fig 4.12   San Diego Trolley: South Bay Transit Ridership

A survey conducted just two months after the Trolley began operation showed that 56 per cent of passengers previously used the bus, 30 per cent used car and 10 per cent did not make the trip (Figure 4.12).

Patronage on the East and South Lines just prior to the opening of the East Line to El Cajon was 29,000 passengers per day. It is currently about 42,000 per day, 28,000 on the South Line and 14,000 on the East Line.

4.5.7   Development and land use

SANDAG (San Diego Association of Governments), the regional planning agency, conducted an impact study which analysed the land use changes between 1980 and 1984. An impact area was defined around the line and the stations.

4.5.7.1 General plans for the area

There was just one change in the general plans involving the trolley impact study, which was to change some industrial designations to residential and to increase the residential densities allowed. This was specifically to recognise the improved accessibility provided by the trolley.

4.5.7.2 Zoning

There were three changes of zoning, though they appeared to be unrelated to the trolley. Overall, very little has been done by local governments to influence development around stations.

4.5.7.3 Building permits

Building permits were analysed as an indicator of construction activity. No permits were issued along the right of way between stations. Some 1200 residential units and 50 commercial projects were processed during the study period. Major developers were identified and asked about the influence of the trolley in their location decisions.

Developers in the city centre generally felt that the trolley was not a key factor in the decision to locate, but it was seen as a valuable factor in marketing the development and in providing transport for staff.

Developers along the suburban section of the line generally indicated that the trolley was an important factor in the location decision. Views were also more favourable about the benefits of the trolley. However, while the benefits of locating closer to the trolley were recognised, on the whole there was very little change in development along the southern line, and none at all in the poorer areas.

4.5.7.4 Survey of local businesses

Local businessmen were asked about the effect of the trolley and 91 responded. About 40 per cent said that the trolley had not affected business. Another 10 per cent had relocated recently and had been attracted by the trolley. A few were moving away because of the restrictions on car access and parking due to the presence of the trolley. Overall, twice the number commented that the trolley was good for business as stated that the trolley damaged their business.

4.5.8   Conclusions

The primary purpose of the trolley was to provide a good public transport service in the face of ever increasing traffic. It was built very economically and covers almost all of its operating costs. It has been widely acclaimed as a successful system and rightly so. The area is experiencing growth and the CBD is being developed rapidly. However, the trolley has as yet had only a marginal effect on that process. Further out along the suburban lines, the benefits of locating close to the trolley are recognised, but have so far given rise to few new developments. The fact that there is no restraint on the use of cars outside the CBD must undermine the advantages of the trolley to potential developers. There are more signs of interaction with development on a planned line to the north, which is the first line not to follow a railway alignment. The choice of route has been influenced by the desire to enhance new development.

4.6   Sacramento, California

4.6.1   The urban area

Sacramento is the capital of California and the fourth largest metropolitan area in the state. It lies at the confluence of the American and Sacramento Rivers, an area of rich croplands. The urban area extends eastward towards the foothills of the Sierra Nevada range. It is about 80 miles north-east of San Francisco and, although it is the base for state legislators and bureaucrats, has been considered to be much less important. Some 25 per cent of the downtown employment is related to State employment. The population is about 335,000 and is rising. The central area is experiencing growth, with new office and hotel buildings.

Sacramento was the western end of the first transcontinental railway and had horse drawn buses in 1858, followed by horse drawn trams and battery trams before getting an electric tramway system in 1895. This lasted until 1947. Public Transport was taken over by the city in 1955. In 1973, a state sales tax was introduced to provide investment in public transport and ridership increased following the improvements.

Population density is low at an average of about 2 dwellings per acre. Car ownership is high. Parking is cheap and abundant in the vicinity of the CBD. About 4 per cent of motorised trips are by public transport. The CBD is fairly small and employs a high proportion of the workers in the higher socio-economic groups. This adds up to an unlikely situation in which to introduce an rapid transit system.

4.6.2   Development of the system

In the mid-1970s, concern began to be expressed by the community about the effect of the rapidly expanding freeway programme on the development of the area. The growth of the city to the north-west between freeways I80 and I50 was a particular cause for concern.

Several freeway proposals were cancelled as a result of political pressure. This provided the opportunity for a group of rail enthusiasts who had formed the Modern Transit Society of Sacramento to propose a historic tramway for the downtown area. The City Council considered the proposal in 1975 and subsequently commissioned a study by consultants which concluded that there was scope for a light rail system with feeder buses. Gradually the idea gained support, although it did not progress much further until it found a strong advocate in Adriana Gianturco, Director of the California Department of Transportation. Rather fortuitously, a sum of $98 million had been allocated to improving the I80 freeway by adding a 5.2 mile bypass and the means existed to transfer these funds to build a light rail system. In August 1979, the political pressure from the state and from numerous community groups finally led the City Council to vote in favour of light rail for the north east corridor. Soon after, the possibility of light rail along the Folsom corridor was also considered. In 1980, the City Council accepted Gianturco's proposal to include both corridors. The draft environmental impact study was published in 1981. Although UMTA were less than enthusiastic about the scheme, the administration agreed to the transfer of the highway funds.

There are three extensions envisaged in Sacramento County. These are fundable under the half per cent sales tax assuming 50 per cent of the costs are received through federal grants. In addition there is also an extension to the airport being examined for funding by means of an assessment district which is basically a tax on the local development. There are just twelve land owners involved and residential development is expected to amount to about 60,000 to 70,000 people so that there is an opportunity for raising private capital. The systems planning for these and other potential extensions is under way and federal funding will be applied for.

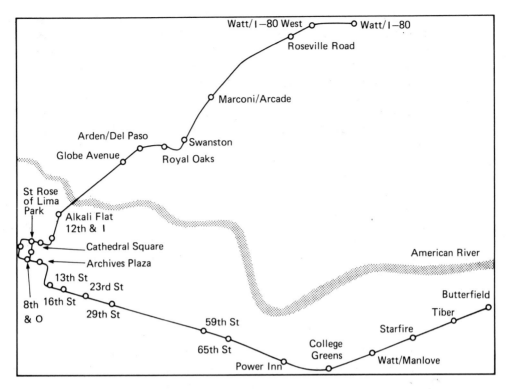

Fig 4.13   Sacramento Light Railway

Sixty per cent of the system (Figure 4.13) is on single track, 40 per cent on double track. Priorities at the moment are towards double tracking the system.

4.6.3   Costs and funding

The original cost was $131m and this was funded by a federal interstate highway transfer by diverting the money allocated for freeway development. UMTA have been against the proposal from the start but could do little to prevent the system being built as the funds were made available. A Sacramento Development Transit Agency (STDA) was created as an agency specifically to build the tramway. The state was initially involved in the Agency following a move of the state highway department to be more involved in transit. However, gradually the state withdrew support and finally STDA was turned over to Regional Transit. The final cost of the system was $176m.

There is no local subsidy for the operation of the system. Fares cover between 28 and 30 per cent of the overall network cost. State subsidies cover the rest of the cost.

Since November 1988 there has been an additional half per cent sales tax of which 35 per cent goes to transit. This amounts to between $14m and $16m a year. The sales tax was originally rejected in June 1988 by voters but subsequently passed in November 1988 after a developers' tax had been introduced to cover the cost of additional infrastructure. The voters had been worried

F

about the sales tax being used to fund more freeway development and therefore increase air pollution and congestion.

The highway development fee was introduced in Sacramento County, rather than the City. When a developer wishes to build a new development there is a one-off payment based on the expenses for building roads and worked out through trip generation. The fee also includes an element for future maintenance and for air pollution measures. In August 1988, a transit development fee was added. This was effective from October 1988. Regional Transit expect to get $23m over ten years through this source.

4.6.4   Patronage

When the system opened in September 1987 it carried 9,700 passengers per day. The forecast number of passengers was 20,500 for the opening day. Patronage has since risen to 19,200 unlinked passenger trips per day. It was planned to have four car sets on the north east corridor with two car sets on the east line. However, patronage has not increased significantly on the north east line, the main increase being on the east line.

4.6.5   Development and land use

Considerable efforts have been made to enhance the pedestrian environment around the line in the city centre. However, the cost of this work was underestimated and the state is now trying to get more money to improve the area. What has been done so far is quite attractive. There are incentives for developers building near the tramway. If building is within 600 metres the developers are required to provide less parking space. A transportation management ordinance has been introduced to reduce car trips by 20 per cent. Developers are offered incentives by means of a menu of measures which they can use to get planning credits, for example putting a bus shelter outside a development allows a credit of 2.5 per cent. Parking fees are going up steadily in the city but the money is not being used to help transit. The transit share is only 1.5 per cent of all trips. There are just 193 buses in Sacramento to serve a population of 950,000.

A development review has been initiated by Regional Transit. This involves monitoring the changes in development around the line and will take some time to complete. The downtown area is booming with 12,000,000 square metres of office space and 820,000 square metres of commercial space. In the areas outside the downtown there are fewer signs of development, apart from the large expanding residential area. This, however, lies in the area between the two lines rather than following either, and is the area where expansion would naturally take place, given the geographical constraints. The transit lines were, in any case, chosen to follow highway alignments rather than being sited so as to encourage development.

The conclusion from Sacramento is that although there are substantial incentives to developers to locate near the transit line, it is only in the city centre where there is any noticeable effect, and even there the transit line is only one influence in an overall climate of rapid development.

4.7   Other cities in the USA

There are a number of other modern rapid transit systems in the USA which were not covered by the TRRL study. Brief details of some of these systems are given here, compiled from available literature. Generally, unless a specific study has been carried out, details of the effects of the systems on urban development are not readily available.

4.7.1   San Francisco, California

The Bay Area Rapid Transit system (BART) in San Francisco (population 2.5 million) opened in five stages between 1972 and 1974. It comprises 115 km of segregated track on 4 lines. 37.4 km of track is in tunnel, 37 km elevated and 40.6 km at grade. The system can be classified at the heavy end of rapid transit, since it serves some of the functions of a suburban railway, like the London Underground but unlike the lighter metros in Lyon, Marseille or Atlanta.

The scheme was primarily funded by the public sector and cost $1.6 billion, of which $942 million was funded by US Bonds (to be repaid by property and sales tax), $176 million by toll revenues, $315 million by federal grants and $186 million from interest and other sources.

The ridership in 1975 was 32 million journeys and by 1986 had risen to 58.9 million journeys. Revenues do not cover operating costs.

The estimated cost of the scheme in 1962 was less than $1 billion. Patronage was forecast for 1975 at 65 million journeys per year.

San Francisco also has an on-street tramway system (the Muni), as well as its famous cable cars.

A major study of the effects of BART on transport, the environment, lifestyles and urban development was carried out during the 1970s (Metropolitan Transit Commission, 1979). It concluded that BART had provided increased transportation capacity with a minimum of environmental disruption. It absorbed most of the increase in commuter traffic in the two busiest corridors into San Francisco and Oakland, and thereby permitted a larger volume of travel to these cities than would have been possible without increased traffic congestion or other additional travel facilities.

BART's impacts on the location of retail establishments was slight, and there were few permanent effects on property prices and rents.

BART's most notable land use impacts occurred in the downtown areas of San Francisco and Oakland, where public policies and market demand helped to encourage the location of new office buildings in the station areas. The system helped maintain the economic stability of the traditional city centres by encouraging some firms to remain and influencing the decisions of a few firms to locate in the city centres. The system also influenced the timing and location of some new residential projects.

No region-wide impacts on development patterns occurred during the first five years of BART.

However, within the counties served by BART, employment increased most rapidly in the narrow corridors along BART lines.

The study concluded that in many cases BART's influence on urban development could not be isolated from other factors. In some instances BART's impacts worked together with other influences to produce land-use changes. For example, in downtown San Francisco office development occurred as a result of civic improvements and zoning changes as well as the BART service. In other locations any potential BART impacts were precluded by other factors. For example, in areas with little commercial activity and where housing was deteriorating, or where the station was isolated form activity centres, there was little likelihood of new developments, and none occurred. In general, the BART experience illustrated the importance of placing rail transit facilities in areas with good development potential to achieve land-use changes.

4.7.2   Cleveland, Ohio

The first portion of the Cleveland transit system, which was opened in 1955, was built on an existing rail right of way. The line ran primarily through established or declining industrial areas and was removed from the direction of new downtown development. This may have essentially neutralised any impetus for significant development generated from the transit system.

Even after the opening of the airport extension in 1968, which provided for an increased scope of service throughout the metropolitan area, there was very little evidence of transit related development. This was partly due to the lack of demand in general, but also because of the absence of pro-development public policies and incentives. The potential role of such policies and incentives was recognised in 1975, when air rights were leased above the station parking lot at the eastern terminal point of the transit system. However, the developer was never able to secure financing and nothing was ever built. Similarly, air rights granted at sites along the airport extension spurred developer interest, but by 1977 no development had yet occurred, due largely to zoning delays.

4.7.3   Portland, Oregon

The Portland light rail system was opened in September 1986 and comprises 15.1 miles of track and 27 stations. The system has both segregated and on-street sections.

The scheme was justified on the grounds that it would reduce car congestion, improve access to the CBD, change land use patterns and enhance and maintain the overall image of the region. It was primarily funded by the public sector at a total cost of $317 million (1982 prices). The Federal Transit Fund contributed $122 million, Federal Road Transfer Fund $144 million, State of Oregon $23.5 million, Oregon Department of Transport $11.5 million, Trimetro the operator, $13 million and local funding $3 million. Payroll, property and sales taxes helped contribute towards the funding of this scheme. The service was designed to provide for approximately 16.1 million journeys per year. Actual patronage for 1986 was 7.23 million journeys.

A Transit Investment Corporation was formed to manage mixed-use joint developments around stations and to encourage the input of private capital through various public improvements such as skybridges and open space enhancements. The board has stimulated more than 2.5 million square feet of new office and retail construction near the light rail line and expects to spur further growth by providing sewers and assembling vacant land around station sites into unincorporated parts of Multnomah county. A large corporate interest has assembled sizable tracts of land around the Lloyd centre and more mixed use development is expected in this area.

4.7.4   San Jose, California

Phase 1 of the San Jose light rail system opened in 1987 and Phase 2, the city centre section, in spring 1988. Phase 3, the Quadeloupe expressway, is planned to open in 1990. The total length of the one line system when complete will be 31 km. Plans for three extensions exist, one of which will connect the San Jose scheme to the San Francisco BART scheme.

The main justification for the scheme was that it was perceived as being cheaper than heavy rail and carried more passengers than bus. The light rail was planned as the centrepiece of the city's 'downtown' mall, which along with density bonuses and landscaping improvements, is expected to stimulate retail and office growth. However San Jose has an unusually small downtown for a city of its size and a wide assortment of development incentives, along with the light rail, appears necessary for a major downtown transformation. Outside the CBD development possibilities could be physically restricted by two new expressways which flank much of the light rail corridor.

The total cost of the scheme was forecast to be $276 million, but the actual cost was $560 million. The federal authority is to contribute 80 per cent of capital costs for the Quadeloupe corridor extension, the remaining 20 per cent is to be funded from state and local taxes (sales and fuel). 50 per cent of the operating costs are expected to be recovered from the fare-box.

The patronage forecast figures vary for the 'downtown' section from 5,000 to 40,000 journeys per day. The actual journey rates have been recorded at 11,000 per day.

4.7.5   Seattle, Washington

The rapid transit scheme in Seattle (population 1.3 million) opened in 1982 and comprises 1.6 km of track on two lines. The system is an elevated monorail. The scheme was built to serve the "World's Fair" site and links the downtown area of Seattle with the "Seattle Centre", a culture and pleasure area.

The scheme was justified on the grounds that it would serve an expanding economy, there was a public acceptance of rapid transit and a lack of public support for highway projects. Petrol and motor vehicle taxes were used to raise revenue for the scheme. Fares (85 per cent) and other commercial sources cover all operating costs.

Patronage for 1982 was 0.73 million, for 1983 1.7 million and for 1985 1.5 million journeys.

4.7.6　Miami, Florida

The rapid transit system in Miami (population 1.7 million) was opened in 1984 and comprises one line with 34.5 km of track and 20 stations. The system is elevated and of metro type. The total cost of the scheme was $900 million.

In 1985 patronage was forecast to be 86 million journeys per year. The actual patronage for 1986 was 6.8 million journeys.

5 Rapid transit systems in Canada

5.1 Canadian policies towards funding public transport

In Canada, the funding of public transport improvements is generally the responsibility of the Province, rather than the national Government. Calgary and Edmonton are both in the Province of Alberta. Toronto lies in the Province of Ontario and Montreal is in Quebec. All costs within this section are in Canadian dollars.

5.1.1 Province of Alberta

The policy of the provincial government is "to provide assistance to cities for capital and operating costs incurred in the development and operation of effective roadway and public transit systems." (Alberta Annual Report 87/88). All of the provincial share for city transportation funding comes from the general revenue fund, which amounted to C$167 million in 1987/88. There are no special taxes in Alberta such as sales tax. The level of control from the Province is less in Alberta than, for example, in Ontario where the Province exerts strong provincial control over spending on cost-shared projects. Despite claims by cities in Alberta that they are constrained to spend money in certain ways, there is a great deal of flexibility in the way in which they can allocate capital resources for transportation investment.

There are five main provincial programmes for supporting transportation. The first is the Basic Capital Programme. City authorities currently receive C$65 per capita per year for funding transportation capital projects. This amounts to around C$40 million each for Calgary and for Edmonton, and may be spent on urban transportation, rapid transit, buses or freeways. The municipality decides how the spending should be allocated between transportation projects. The Province decides whether the projects in the list are eligible and provides advice to the local authority before approving the programme. The Province then pays 75 per cent of the costs of local projects, leaving 25 per cent to be found locally, so the C$40 million represents around C$52 million worth of work in 1989.

The second programme is the Primary Highways Connectors Programme. Highways which are identified by the Province as being of provincial importance are funded through grants. C$16 million was available in 1989 for grants at 75 per cent level.

Thirdly, there is the Public Transit Operating Programme. There are 2 levels of funding from the Province. The first is a C$2.94 per capita per year for elderly and disabled people and the other is C$7.84 per capita per year for municipalities which operate bus or rail transit systems. In the two conurbations of Calgary and Edmonton, around 40-45 per cent of operating costs is covered by fare-box revenue, and a further 6-7 per cent of costs is covered by these grants. In the more rural areas 20-25 per cent of operating costs is covered by revenue and 45 per cent of the operating costs by the provincial grant.

The other two grants are the Community Safe Streets grant, which provides C$5 per capita for construction of safety related capital projects at 75 per cent cost-sharing, and the Primary Highway Maintenance grant which provides C$1959 per lane-kilometre of primary highway under the city's jurisdiction.

Despite the similarity in the population and capital funding of Calgary and Edmonton, there are significant differences in the progress of the Calgary and Edmonton light rail systems. Calgary started 3 years after Edmonton. However, there are now three lines operational whereas Edmonton is currently working on its second. This is primarily due to a decision to go underground through the Edmonton city centre which has proved to be more expensive, and the city of Edmonton also decided not to overspend available sources of funding. Over half of the current capital spending in Edmonton is currently on the light rail line. This has meant that other transportation projects have been decelerated while it has been under construction.

There are 17 cities in Alberta of which 10 have transit systems and just 2 have LRT. The population of the entire Edmonton area is 650,000, that of Calgary is 670,000 and the next largest community has a population of 60,000.

5.1.2   Quebec province

In the late 1970s the government of Quebec was concerned at the loss of good agricultural land for building. Each municipality was trying to attract development by providing infrastructure and all were asking for money.

An urban development planning process was introduced in 1979. This involved several levels of plan and required provincial approval. The final stage of this process would include by-laws to determine the size, density and scale of development. The provincial plan for Montreal was to consolidate within the urban framework and to build on existing sites without substantial further investment on highways.

The Montreal Urban Community did not share the same views and is was not until 1987 that the first plan for Montreal was produced.

Meanwhile the provincial government had changed direction and in 1985 relaxed its policy regarding the green belt. More recently still, following 10-15 years of resisting highway development, there has been a renewed interest in road building.

The first phase of the Metro was initiated by Montreal itself, but after one year, the Province took over 60 per cent of the capital costs. Grants of 10-30 per cent for new buses were introduced in 1976. In 1980, these grants were extended to other public transport infrastructure and increased to 75 per cent. At the same time, the Province took over paying the total capital cost of future extensions to the subway system.

With an increase in provincial spending on the subway came a slowing down of investment and there have been several reviews of the proposals. A package of extensions amounting to C$1,000 million has been considered and is waiting for provincial approval at present.

5.2   Calgary, Alberta

5.2.1   The urban area

Calgary is a city of 670,000 people situated near the base of the Rocky Mountains. It grew initially as an agricultural and ranching centre and still retains a strong agricultural business base. The annual Calgary Exhibition and Stampede, held in July, is a world famous event. Recently, Calgary has developed as the headquarters city of the Canadian Oil and Gas Industry.

The central downtown core is situated at the confluence of the rivers Bow and Elbow and is very concentrated. There is a broad band of industrial land which runs north/south on the eastern side of the city and extensive residential development to the north, west and south. The city gives the impression of being well planned. Major roads running north/south and east/west divide the city neatly into blocks and the new areas are developed following servicing with major roads.

5.2.2   The development of the system

In the late 1970s Calgary was undergoing dramatic expansion. Most of the major oil companies had head offices there and development in the downtown area was expanding. There were plans for several new tower blocks. However, this expansion gave rise to concern about the increasing problems of congestion on the roads and developers were being driven to look for sites outside the downtown area to develop new facilities. The rapid transit was seen as a solution to getting people to the downtown area while relieving congestion. Around 100,000 jobs are in the downtown area out of a total population in the city of 670,000, a very high proportion.

The first line of the C-Train rapid transit system (Figure 5.1) was the South line. This ran along 7th Avenue South, in the downtown area and then turned south along the right of way of an existing Canadian Pacific Railway line. The eleven single direction stations along the 1.2 mile 7th Avenue are more closely spaced through the downtown area than along the rest of the line, with 7 stations in 6.6 miles. Passengers may travel free anywhere along 7th Avenue, which was reserved solely for buses before the rapid transit which now shares the roadway with buses. The South line serves the Stampede Grounds where the Calgary Stampede is held and then travels between the residential areas to the west and the industrial areas to the east. The line ends at Anderson Station in the residential suburbs to the south. In common with other systems which use an existing right of way, there is quite a wide physical separation between the line and other land uses.

The second line to be built was the northeast line which was opened in April 1985. This line follows 7th Avenue through the city centre, then continues east through the wide belt of industrial land, which includes Calgary Zoo, before turning north between the industrial zone to the west and residential estates to the east. For most of its length, the line runs down the centre of major arterial roadways. The line is 6 miles in length.

The third line, the Northwest Line, runs out to the northwest for 3.3 miles as far as the University. A further 0.8km extension to Brentwood is currently under construction and should be open in 1990. This line was an important feature of the 1988 Winter Olympics as it serves several large

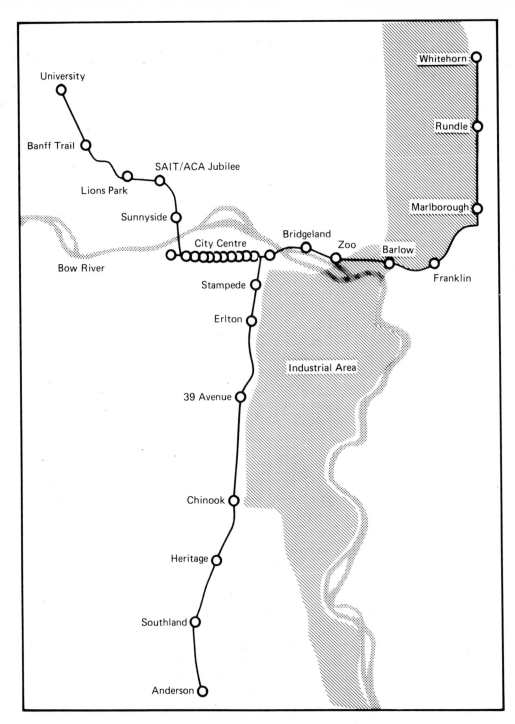

Fig 5.1   Calgary C-Train

complexes, such as the McMahon Stadium, the speed-skating oval and the University of Calgary, which were important Olympic venues. Most of the line runs through long established residential areas and there was considerable difficulty in gaining the acceptance of the light rail by the three communities directly affected by it. Indeed, in an effort to appease these communities special liaison committees were established with a C$4m budget to spend on improving the design of the light rail stations and structures to make them more acceptable to the communities. The Northwest Line opened in September 1987.

The total length of the system, built so far, is 17.3 miles with 19 major stations and 11 single direction platforms in the downtown area.

There are long term plans for extending all three existing legs as well as new legs to the north, west and south east. If and when these new legs get built is very much dependent upon the future prosperity and rate of growth of the City.

5.2.3   Costs and funding

The south line, which was built during the boom, cost C$174 million. The northeast line cost C$203 million and the northwest line cost C$104 million; these lines were built during the recession when construction costs were much lower. With the integrated nature of funding for transport infrastructure in Alberta, it is difficult to compare these costs with costs elsewhere. For example, the costs associated with some of the associated highway construction are included in all of these cost figures.

The operating cost of all public transport in Calgary was C$83 million in 1988. Total fare-box revenue was C$40.9 million, 49 per cent of the costs.

5.2.4   Patronage

The system carries 99,000 passengers per day, or 28 million per year. The south line carries 33,000 passengers, the northwest line 20,000, the northeast line 26,000 and the downtown area 20,000.

5.2.5   Development and land use

Calgary experienced a boom in development in the late 1970s. There were plans for numerous developments and so the city planning department conducted studies and began to develop policies for channelling the new development.

The last recession, which was prolonged in Alberta by the 1986 collapse in oil prices, had a dramatic affect. House prices fell by as much as 30 per cent and have still not fully recovered. The population of the city dropped radically and much of the planned development was never started.

Along the south line of the rapid transit careful consideration had been given to the creation of planning districts around each station with conditions to channel development in the fashion desired by the planners. However the downturn in the economy meant that many of these planned developments never took place and it also meant that there were a large number of vacant sites in the central area which have since been used for car parking.

The easy access to car parking has had a further detrimental effect on the rapid transit. Whereas prices for parking in the days of the boom were 100 dollars a month, with the recession the cost of parking in the downtown area became less than the cost of a monthly transit pass.

The reduction in the pressure for development has resulted in a gradual loss of political will to implement the strong planning measures conceived in a different climate. An amendment to the Calgary Municipal Plan stated "While it is generally recognised that supportive residential and office development in the station areas contributes towards the efficient utilisation of the system, however it is important to stress that it is not city policy that high development densities would automatically accompany the LRT system. The LRT land use strategy must strive to achieve a sensitive balance between the protection of communities, and the skilful accommodation of an appropriate level of supportive development."

Two studies have been done on the impact of the C-Train. A study of the south line examined a large number of light rail related proposed developments which had been approved between 1979 and 1982. However, most of these have not yet been built. The rapid decline in demand for property in 1981 and 1982 and therefore in land values effectively swamped any effect of the light rail in encouraging development.

The Northwest LRT Impact Monitoring Study is a much more comprehensive examination of the effects of light rail than the study done on the south line. The northwest study not only looked at the actual changes which had occurred in terms of land use, property values, demographics etc, but documented the public's perception of the impact of light rail before the line was built for comparison with the public's view of the line when it had been in operation for two or more years.

There is much less scope for new development along the northeast and northwest lines and they have been opened for much less time so there are no development effects of significance along these lines.

5.3   Edmonton, Alberta

5.3.1   The urban area

The city of Edmonton itself has a population of 580,000 but with satellite cities the metropolitan area population is around 650,000. Calgary and Edmonton are therefore of similar size, and are similar in many other ways, with common industries. They are both within the Province of Alberta and therefore receive similar amounts of funding for transportation investment. They have both introduced light rail transit systems within similar timescales. There are however significant differences which have a bearing on the development of the two light rail systems.

Calgary is by nature a city of headquarters, particularly of oil companies and banks. It is a place prepared to take major financial risks and to invest money in innovative ways; for example the 1988 Olympics gave rise to massive investment in infrastructure.

Edmonton, on the other hand, is a more industrial centre - it contains the oil refineries and associated industries. It has more blue collar workers. Edmonton also has a major University campus which for many purposes can be regarded as a sub-centre. The area is more conservative and this is reflected in the investment policies. The industrial areas in Edmonton are more dispersed than in Calgary and are placed on the periphery of the city with neighbouring residential areas and so the journey to work pattern is more diffuse. There are still a large number of journeys to the downtown and University areas but the nature of transit operation to the industrial areas is quite difficult.

There is virtually no congestion in Edmonton. For example a journey to work from the northwest suburbs of 12-15 km takes between 28 and 35 minutes which is much the same as 10 years ago. The city relies on traffic lights and traffic management measures to control the flows. As an example of the capacity of Edmonton streets, there was a transit strike in 1983 and during this time when people were using cars the city functioned more or less as normal.

The city operates a timed transfer policy. Buses arrive at 8 major transfer points where they layover for 4 or 5 minutes to allow passengers to interconnect with other services and then depart. The pattern of movement is quite rectangular, following the grid pattern of the city, which is itself rectangular in shape.

In marked contrast to Calgary, there are few Park and Ride facilities associated with Edmonton's light rail line, apart from the last two stations on the line. The reason is that downtown parking is cheap and plentiful at around C$1.5 dollars per day just a few blocks outside the city centre. There are many parking areas due to the large number of sites which were prepared for building prior to the 1981 crash and have never been developed. Developers are allowed to provide less parking if a development is near a light rail station, but they do not necessarily do so.

5.3.2 The development of the system

The original justification for the light rail line was that the cost of a freeway to the northeast could be offset by investing in a rapid transit system. During the 1960's Edmonton was rapidly developing and plans for the construction of several freeways were prepared. These included not only freeways in the north, south, east and west but in the quadrants in between as well. Light rail emerged as an alternative option to the freeway for less money. The downtown merchants did not want to lose street capacity and with the city being interested in longer term upgrading to a metro type system, the decision was taken to go underground through the city centre with the intention to come up to grade for the line on the south side.

The first phase of the line (Figure 5.2) was built between 1974 and 1978 and opened three years ahead of the Calgary system. The line starts underneath the city's busiest street corner at Central Transit station and then travels east to Churchill station which serves the art gallery, theatre and City Hall. From there the line comes up to the surface and follows the track of the Canadian National Railway out to Belvedere.

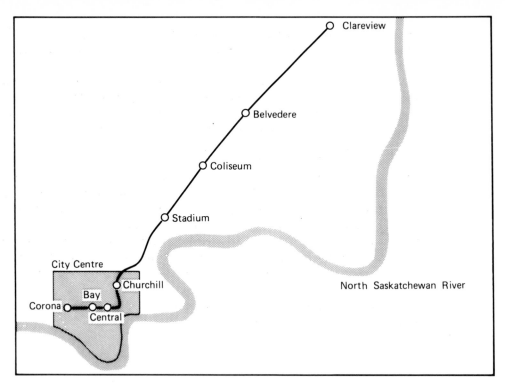

Fig 5.2   Edmonton Light Rail Transit

The line was extended by 2.2 km to Clareview, the current terminus, in 1981. About 30 buses were taken off the north east corridor when the light rail system was introduced. In 1983, two further underground stations opened along Jasper Avenue in the Central Business District.

Difficulties have been encountered in constructing the South line from the Jasper Avenue section across the river to the south. It had been intended to use the High Level railway bridge but problems with agreeing the shared use of this facility meant that the alignment of the line was changed to go into deep tunnel on a different horizontal alignment.

5.3.3   Costs and funding

The cost of the first phase was C$64.9 million, compared to the original estimate of C$66 million. This consisted of the middle five stations, two of which were underground. The system received a provincial grant of C$45 million. The extension of the line by a further station to Clareview cost C$9.2 million. The downtown extension of 0.9 km and a further two underground stations cost C$95.8 million. The total cost of the system to date, including C$30 million for the tram depot is C$200 million.

The South Line extension now being built across the river to the university will include two more underground stations and will cost C$142.7 million.

In 1988, the total cost of operating the Edmonton public transport system was C$77.1 million, just slightly less than in Calgary. Revenues were C$32.0 million or 42 per cent of operating costs.

Following the 1981 crash the city of Edmonton embarked on a capital debt reduction programme. This established a capital spending limit of C$40 million per year. The Transportation Department received a large proportion of these funds as provincial grants were available at the level of 75 per cent so the city was only required to fund 25 per cent of capital transportation projects.

Of the total funds available for transportation about 25 per cent has been allocated to the light rail system, 20 per cent to maintaining and improving the roadway system, 20 per cent to special projects which are eligible for provincial grants, 20 per cent for major roadways, less than 10 per cent for extending internal roadways into subdivisions and 5 per cent for infrastructure. Edmonton Transit need to replace a large number of buses in 1992 and are going to require between C$8 and C$15 million dollars a year to create a continuous replacement policy. The council would like to speed up the programme of light rail development but is unwilling to take any further money from other transportation projects. These projects have to some extent already suffered through the requirement for investment in light rail. At the moment the council is trying to find some additional money to speed up the development of light rail. The system is being extended in small steps and it is thought that it will be some considerable time before the council will approve larger sections of line again.

The corporate debt of Edmonton is around C$250 million compared with C$1.6 billion dollars for Calgary. By 1997 the corporate debt will be cleared and Edmonton expects to be able to increase the budget for light rail to C$70 million per year.

5.3.4   Patronage

The line carries about 25,000 passengers a day, about a quarter of that carried by the Calgary system, and transit use generally is going down. There is a total fleet of 700 buses of which 580 are used in the peak. Calgary in contrast puts out fewer buses for fewer hours.

5.3.5   Development and land use

At the same time as making the decision to build the line, the city council also decided not to support development around stations except for plans for massive development at the end of the line around Clareview. They zoned out the capability of development elsewhere by land use by-laws.

However, following the economic crash in 1981 the grand plans for Clareview area have been withdrawn and at the same time there is some interest from developers and from members of the council in supporting increased densities, for example apartments, near stations. This has been the first time there has been any interest in apartments anywhere, let alone near the light rail line.

The line has two quite distinct parts - the underground section which runs through the central business district and the surface line which follows the track of the Canadian National railway. While there are signs of new development in the downtown area, it would be difficult to attribute these to the light rail. Conversely, the general policy of the city council and the wide separation of the surface line from the neighbouring development provides only limited scope for development along the suburban part of the line.

5.4   Toronto, Ontario

5.4.1   The urban area

Toronto is the primary financial, administrative and service centre of Ontario and Canada. The urban area is situated on the northern bank of Lake Ontario and covers an area 24 miles wide by 10 miles deep. It began as a trading post which had grown to a population of 9000 when given the status of a city in 1834. The municipality of Metropolitan Toronto has a present population of about 2 million people.

The Toronto region accounts for twenty per cent of the jobs in Canada, compared with a population of 12.5 per cent. Approximately 40 per cent of the head offices of the top 500 Canadian companies are located in the region. Currently, 76 per cent of the employment in Metropolitan Toronto is in the service sector.

During the period 1976-85, the Toronto area experienced an annual rate of employment growth of 3-4 per cent, much of it in the areas around Metropolitan Toronto. Population is expected to increase by around 1 per cent per annum until the year 2001. The diversity of employment opportunities continues to attract new residents to the area. The economy exhibits a high level of growth and innovation which benefits the region as a whole.

5.4.2   Development of public transport

Public transport arrived in Toronto in the shape of horse-drawn carriages along Yonge Street, the main North/South street, in 1849. By 1861 the city had grown to 45,000 when the Toronto Street Railway Company opened tramlines along Yonge Street, Queen Street and King Street. By 1891, the system had expanded to 68 miles of track and was carrying 55,000 people per day. In the next twenty years, the population of Toronto doubled to 350,000 people. In 1921, the tramways were taken into public ownership and a massive programme of expansion and upgrading was started by the Toronto Transportation Commission. Between 1921 and 1953 there was steady expansion and investment in buses, tramcars and trolley buses.

The Toronto Transit Commission was established in 1954 with responsibility for the whole of the newly created Metropolitan Toronto area. This expanded the public transport system from an area of 35 square miles to 244 square miles.

The first subway line opened along Yonge Street in 1954 and the system has been continually expanded since then. The current public transport system consists of tramways including the original ones in King Street and Queen Street and almost every other conceivable form of public transport - 1,597 conventional buses, 90 articulated buses, 662 subway cars, 139 trolley coaches,

37 PCC streetcars, 52 Advanced Light Rail Vehicles (ALRVs), 196 Canadian Light Rail Vehicles (CLRVs), 28 Intermediate Capacity Transit System (ICTS) vehicles for the Scarborough RT and 123 Wheel-Trans buses. The system carried 463.5 million passengers in 1988.

Public Transport is fully integrated between all modes. Routes tend to follow the rectangular pattern of streets in the city, running either north/south or east/west and so it is easy to understand. It is also cheap to use. There is a computerised inquiry system which provides information by telephone for each of the 9000 transit stops. By 1974, 95 per cent of the population were within 600 metres of a service. The public transport system is very stable - a service has been running down Yonge Street for 140 years! It is helped by the continuous dense and varied pattern of development and comparatively narrow streets. The highway network is quite heavily congested with traffic despite the construction of good urban freeways.

5.4.3   The rapid transit

The origin of the subway was quite simply the need for increased capacity to cope with demand. Yonge Street was the first public transport route and has continued to be a crucial spine up to the present.

The story of how the subway developed covers a period of 35 years and is complex; only a short summary will be presented here. The single most important aspect is the consistent high priority given to public transport, backed up by expansion and investment. For example, the Prince Edward Viaduct which opened across the Don Valley in 1918 included a lower deck for a subway - the subway opened 48 years later!

The first line (Figure 5.3) was a short north/south section of 4.6 miles of the Yonge Street line from Eglinton to Union. In 1963, a further 2.4 miles extended the line from Union to St George's, forming a U in the downtown area. In 1966, the central 8.0 miles of the Bloor/Danforth line opened between Woodbine to the East and Keele to the West. This line was originally to run further South, but the expansion of the city northwards made Bloor Street more central. There are still six tramway lines (Numbers 501-506) running parallel to and south of the Bloor/Danforth line through the city centre.

In May 1968, the Bloor/Danforth line was extended by 6.1 miles to run from Warden in the east to Islington. The eastern arm of the Yonge line was extended northwards by 2.7 miles to York Mills in 1973 and by another 2.7 miles in 1974 to Finch, the current terminus. The portion of the western arm of the U north of Bloor Street was named the Spadina Line and this opened from St George's to Wilson, a distance of 6.2 miles in 1978. A further station was added to each end of the Bloor/Danforth line in November 1980, these two extensions amounting to 2.6 miles.

The most recent extension has been the Scarborough Rapid Transit (RT) which runs from the eastern terminus of the Bloor/Danforth line a distance of 4.1 miles out to Scarborough town centre. The system uses different technology from the rest of the subway, being powered by linear induction motors, and it is fully automatic. Although the trains have operators, their sole task in "driving" the train normally is to press a button to signal the train to proceed to the next station. The system was developed by UTDC and its operation is partially funded by a special grant from the Province of Ontario. The Scarborough RT opened in March, 1985.

91

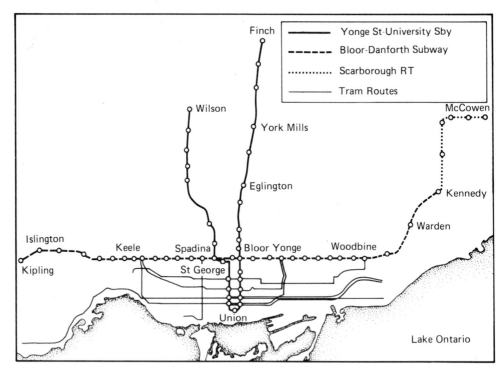

Fig 5.3   Toronto Rapid Transit Network

5.4.4   Costs and funding

Under the current method of funding, the operating costs are based on a 'user's fair share' agreement under which the Commission aims to provide 68 per cent of total costs through revenues. The Province provides a subsidy based on a complicated formula which on average provides 16 per cent of costs. The remainder is provided by the municipality of Metropolitan Toronto. In 1988, the operating subsidy amounted to C$150.4 million out of a total cost of C$531.9 million.

Funding of the capital costs of the line has changed over the period of almost 40 years since construction of the subway began. The TTC paid for the first section of line directly. However, increasing public assistance has been required ever since. The cost of the east/west line was funded based on a complicated formula which resulted in the municipality paying for approximately 55 per cent of the cost. The east/west extensions approved in 1963 was funded on another complicated formula which resulted in a 70 per cent grant from Metropolitan Toronto. From 1964, the Province of Ontario provided a grant of 33 per cent for right-of-way construction. For the most recent extension to the Yonge Street line, Metropolitan Toronto took responsibility for the total cost and in the meanwhile, the Province increased the level of grant to 50 per cent of all the costs. By 1972, this had risen to 75 per cent of total costs and this is still in effect. The Spadina portion of the Yonge/Spadina Line and the extension to the Bloor-Danforth Line was funded 75 per cent by the Province and 25 per cent by Metropolitan Toronto. Capital expenditure in 1988 amounted to C$138.1 million of which the Province paid C$101.5 million and the municipality paid C$27.3 million, leaving C$9.3 million to be paid by TTC.

In addition, TTC receives 87 per cent of the costs of the Scarborough System under a special funding arrangement. The total construction cost of the Scarborough RT was C$196 million.

Until 1972, the financing of all other surface transport capital assets was the responsibility of TTC. From that date, the Province has provided 75 per cent grants for eligible capital acquisitions which include new buses, trolley buses and rapid transit vehicles.

5.4.5 Patronage

In 1988, the subway carried 994,000 revenue and transfer passengers per average business day, which is 38 per cent of the total public transport trips. Overall, there were 463.5 million passengers in the entire system in 1988 and this had been increasing steadily since 1978.

5.4.6 Development and land use

It has been claimed that the Toronto public transport system is the best in the world; it is certainly very impressive, has a very high level of public confidence and is well used. But then the city provides an abundant mixture of cultural and entertainment facilities which attracts people all through the day.

When the Yonge Street line opened, shopkeepers near to Metro stations benefited from an increase in shoppers, while those between stations complained about loss of business. However, the benefits of being close to the subway spread right along Yonge Street. The effects of the subway on development have followed same pattern and are famous. High rise development can be seen around stations towering above the surrounding area. Half of all apartment construction within the thirty year period 1954-84 occurred within a five minute walk of rapid transit stations and 90 per cent of all office construction in the same period occurred adjacent to downtown stations or at Bloor, St Clair and Eglinton Stations.

Many of the new developments in the city centre are directly linked into the subway. There are extensive underground walkways which connect buildings and the subway together.

The conditions for suburban office development in Toronto have been particularly favourable. The ever increasing demand for offices in the central area has pushed up rents. This has probably created a secondary demand for high quality offices in the suburban centres which are cheaper, but have good transportation links. According to the Metropolitan Plan Review produced by the municipality, there are types of companies which provide services to larger companies (e.g. Chartered accountants, lawyers, engineering consultants) who prefer to locate in suburban centres. The high quality transportation system in Toronto makes it possible for these companies to be in close touch with their customers.

There are some joint developments. At York Mills, a developer is extending a block of offices and shops to encompass the existing station, which has been redesigned as part of the complex. A new bus interchange is being built into the development which is the subject of a complex agreement between TTC and the developer. Bus and subway passengers will enter the station through the new shopping development.

Toronto would appear to be a success story in terms of development effects, but there are a number of caveats that need to be made before trying to transfer these results elsewhere.

The investment in public transport in Toronto has been vast and has placed an increasing strain on the public purse. Early subway lines were easily justified in terms of demand, but the cases for further extension get more difficult as the costs rise and the additional generated patronage gets smaller. The annual operating subsidy of C$150 million and capital costs of C$130 million for 1988 can more easily be justified within an expanding economy such as Toronto, but this may not be so elsewhere.

The attractive lifestyle of the city attracts people - the extremely expensive new harbourfront apartments are just one example of this. The transport system and these activities are interdependent on each other and have been built up incrementally over a period of 150 years. The stability of public transport as part of the planning of the city has provided the confidence for the development, which in turn has helped the public transport system. Toronto has enjoyed a long period of tremendous growth and prosperity which has fuelled the pace of change. Such conditions are unlikely to occur elsewhere.

While developers have entered into agreements with TTC for access to new developments, they have not, in the main, been asked to contribute in a major way towards the subway costs. The transport investment is seen by the municipality as a means of attracting development and there have been additional incentives, such as high floor area ratios near to stations, to persuade developers to build near the subway. The philosophy is that the city will gain from the development in terms of direct and secondary employment as well as through property taxes. If developers had been asked to contribute more, the result may have been less dramatic.

5.5   Montreal, Quebec

5.5.1   The urban area

Montreal Metropolitan region has a population of 2.9 million people, 60 per cent of whom live on the main Montreal island, the largest of several on the Saint Lawrence River. The City is one of 29 communities making up the Montreal Urban Community (CUM), which covers an area of 490 square km. About three quarters of the area is developed. Over the past two decades, there has been a shift of population outwards from the city centre to the suburbs, particularly at the eastern and western ends of the main island.

The central portion of the island accounts for 35 per cent of all the jobs in the region and, contrary to the trend in population, the number of jobs has been increasing. During the morning rush hour, 65 per cent of all trips to downtown Montreal are made by public transport. For the island as a whole, the public transport share of morning trips remained stable between 1974 and 1982 at about 46 per cent. The number of passengers has increased, though the public transport provision has increased more, with commuter trains and bus lanes as well as Metro investment. Transit ridership in Montreal is high at 180 public transport trips per person per year.

The development of the network of expressways began in the late 1950s and continued until the 1970s. The programme was curtailed in 1977 and a number of schemes were delayed or cancelled. As a result the network is incomplete. In 1987, summertime traffic across the bridges amounted to 1 million vehicles per day. There is a real problem of traffic congestion.

Public Transport is operated by the Société de Transport de la Communauté urbaine de Montréal (MUCTC). Operating subsidy for MUCTC is provided by the Montreal Urban Community. The Metro is designed and constructed by the Metropolitan Transit Bureau, which is also funded through the Urban Community.

The newcomer sees a lot in common between Toronto and Montreal. They both are strategic Canadian financial and commercial centres. They have similar planning environments and work within similar provincial policies for supporting public transport. It is interesting then to observe the differences and to try to explain these. Toronto CBD is stronger and larger than that of Montreal, and development has been more rapid. Montreal has some very high quality new buildings, but these are concentrated in the central area and there are inner areas in dire need of investment. Public transport in Toronto and, in particular, the subway has had more consistent and stable financing than that in Montreal. The vehicle fleet in Toronto is newer. The freeway programme in Toronto is more advanced. The effect of the subway on development is far less marked in Montreal and there are some parts which appear to be unaffected. Although city planning is strong in both centres, the suburban centres which have been a feature of Toronto have not developed in Montreal to the same extent and so there are particular problems with commuting into the city.

5.5.2   The development of the subway

The idea of a Metro for Montreal had been considered for some years, but the decision to authorise construction of the first two lines was taken by Mayor Drapeau in 1961. Although the city of Montreal initiated construction, provincial funding of 60 per cent of the construction costs was agreed after one year.

The initial system consisted of line 1 which ran for 6 km east-west through the centre and line 2, which ran parallel to line 1 through the centre and then turned north to the northern shore of the island. These two sections opened in 1966 (Figure 5.4).

The system is entirely underground, mostly in bored tunnel with some cut and cover construction. The vehicles are the same as those used in Paris with rubber wheels for quiet operation and good adhesion. The line slopes up as it approaches each station and down as it leaves to assist with the acceleration and deceleration of the train. Approximately 8 per cent of power is saved by this method. The Montreal trains travel at a top speed of 82 km/hour compared with 60 km/hour for the Paris Metro.

Following the decision to hold Expo 67 in Montreal, a 4.2 km length of line connecting the city centre with Longueil was authorised and this opened in 1967 as line 4.

Between 1981 and 1983 there were many ambitious plans which included upgrading the

95

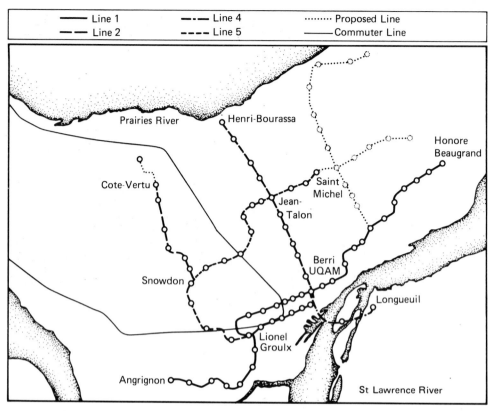

Prairies River

Henri-Bourassa

Honore
Beaugrand

Cote-Vertu

Saint
Michel

Jean-
Talon

Berri
UQAM

Snowdon

Longueuil

Lionel
Groulx

Angrignon

St Lawrence River

Fig 5.4   Montreal Metro

Canadian National railway to a full metro. Subsequently, many of these plans were downgraded or abandoned and, to date, there has been no line 3, although there is a current proposal for one.

Between 1976 and 1978, line 1 was extended to its current termini at Honoré-Beaugrand and Angrignon. Line 2 was steadily extended out from the city centre to the north-west between 1981 and 1986, when the line was completed out to Côte Vertu.

The most recent line, line 5, runs parallel to the city centre lines, but further north. The first part opened in 1986 from Saint Michel to Castelnau, including an interchange with line 2 at Jean-Talon station. This was extended to link with the western arm of line 2 at Snowdon in 1988.

The current network consists of four lines (1,2,4 and 5) with a total of 61 km and 65 stations (4 of which are on several lines). The growth of the Metro is shown in Figure 5.5.

There are several plans to extend the system further and these have changed during the last few years. One proposal was to extend line 5 by turning north to Montréal-Nord with six additional stations at a cost of roughly C$200 million. More recently, this has been changed to extend line 5 by five stations and to build a new line 7 from Pie IX on line 1 through an intersection with the extended line 5 and then following a similar track to that of the first proposal. The western end of line 2 is to extended northwards by two stations. This project will include a transfer station with

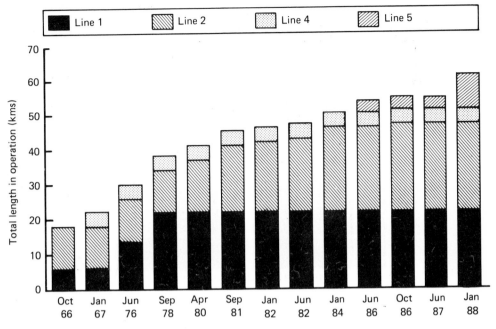

| Line 1 | Line 2 | Line 4 | Line 5 |

Total length in operation (kms)

Fig 5.5   *Growth of Montreal Metro*

the Canadian National commuter line and a new garage and workshop. It will cost around C$100 million.

5.5.3   Regional railways

The role of the STCUM was expanded in 1980 to take over responsibility for two suburban rail lines operated by Canadian National (CN) and Canadian Pacific (CP) railways. These had suffered from lack of investment while the Metro system had been developed. Since then the STCUM, with the help of the provincial government, has been trying to modernise the lines and integrate them with the bus and Metro system. It is planned to convert the CN line from Centrale Station to Deux-Montagnes into a full Metro as line 3. Provincial funding is currently being sought for this conversion.

5.5.4   Patronage

The growth in patronage between 1966 and 1981 is shown in Figure 5.6. This can be viewed against the level of supply of public transport which is shown in Figure 5.7. Current Metro ridership is 221 million passengers per year.

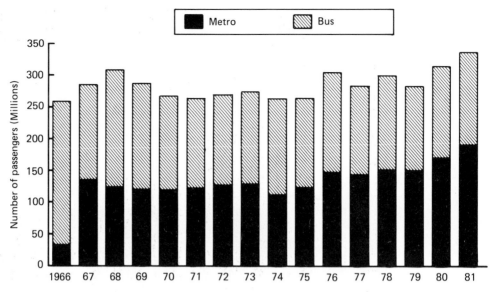

Fig 5.6   *Montreal - Annual Passengers on Bus and Metro*

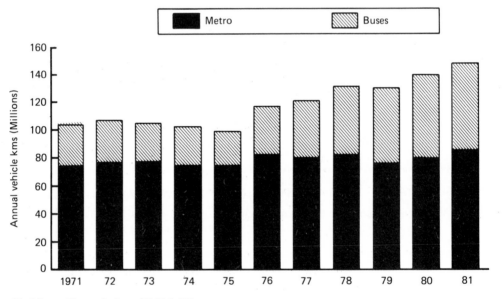

Fig 5.7   *Montreal - Annual Vehicle Kilometres*

5.5.5   Costs and funding

Up to the end of 1987, the complete Metro system had cost C$1,135 million. A profile of costs by year is given in Figure 5.8. The costs for the individual lines were:-

Line 1 C$356 million
Line 2 C$408 million
Line 5 C$371 million

98

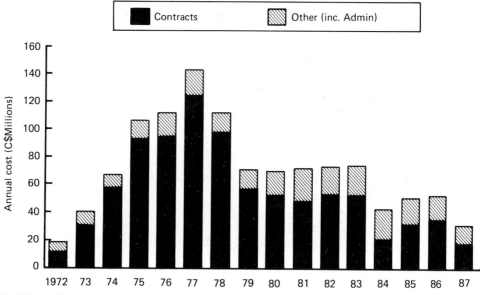

| | Contracts | | Other (inc. Admin) |

Fig 5.8   *Montreal - Costs of building the system*

The first phase of the Metro was initiated by Montreal itself, but after one year, the Province took over 60 per cent of the capital costs. Grants of 10-30 per cent for new buses were introduced in 1976. In 1980, these grants were extended to other public transport infrastructure and increased to 75 per cent. At the same time, the Province took over paying the total capital cost of future extensions to the subway system.

With an increase in provincial spending on the subway came a slowing down of investment and there have been several reviews of the proposals. A package of extensions amounting to C\$1,000 million has been considered and is waiting for provincial approval at present. This includes the upgrading of the CN line to a full Metro (line 3), the extension of line 5 to Montréal-Nord, the extension of line 2 by a further two stations to link with the CN line and new rolling stock. When added to the existing capital commitment, the total bid is for C\$2,500 million.

As the Montreal Metro system is more than twenty years old, the rolling stock need extensive renovation which is estimated to cost C\$60 million. The Metro control and ticket collection are to be modernised and new communication and safety systems are planned. This work has been estimated at about C\$136 million, but has not yet been funded.

5.5.6   Operating costs

Between 1976 and 1979, the Province paid half the operating deficit for the Montreal public transport, leaving the urban community to pay the other half. In 1980 the provincial subsidy was changed to 40 per cent of the revenue. A subsidy was also introduced to reimburse the operator for revenue lost through the introduction of a monthly pass.

These subsidies were reduced during the period 1984-87 by placing a ceiling on the total amount and by reducing the subsidy for the monthly pass. The Province currently pays 35 per cent of the operating costs for Montreal. Revenue covers 40 per cent, leaving the urban community to pay the remaining 24 per cent. This amounted to C$263 million in 1986.

5.5.7   Development and land use

There is a strong European style planning tradition in Montreal. An urban development plan process was introduced in 1979 which was very similar to the 1968 Development Plan process in Britain. It is based on land use plans on different time scales and at different levels of detail. The preliminary development plan must be approved at provincial level. Following this, there are several more detailed plans leading to planning by-laws which specify, for example, the density, type of construction and size of developments which can take place.

The first official plan for Montreal was produced in 1987. This had taken a long time due to differences between the provincial and local governments.

The provincial policies have undergone considerable change. In the late 1970s there was concern about the loss of agricultural land which was being used for development. The emphasis was placed on consolidating the urban fabric by building on existing sites to restrict the growth of highways. However, since 1985 there has been a relaxation of these policies with fewer restrictions on green belt development and a move back towards highway construction.

Population has been moving out of the central areas to lower density development at the eastern and western ends of the island. Property taxes in Montreal are 2-3 times higher than on the south shore and 5 times higher than elsewhere. This is thought to have encouraged people to move out of the city. However, this trend exacerbates the traffic problem by increasing commuting.

The current planning policy in Montreal is to preserve the central area, but also to focus other development in sub-centres similar to those which have developed in Toronto. The city was initially opposed to extensions of the Metro into the suburbs with potential for development as it would attract development away from the centre.

Montreal has a small tightly defined central area. While there are a number of very high quality developments occurring in the centre, particularly around Metro stations, the development has not so far spread out along the lines as has occurred in Toronto. The most spectacular development related to the Metro is the rapidly expanding network of underground thorough-fares. The winter climate in Montreal is severe and this led to the first underground shopping complex at Place Ville-Marie. The present system consists of 22 km of pedestrian walkway. Some 100,000 people work in offices and shops with direct access to the network and the Metro is extremely well integrated with the development. Figure 5.9 shows the extent of the underground system and the direct connections with buildings. The entrances to city centre Metro stations are often also access points to the underground network and are located within existing buildings.

The main reason for the success of the integration between office and shopping developments and the Metro is a powerful planning framework which ensures high architectural standards are maintained. This in turn is in the interests of the developers because the resulting level of

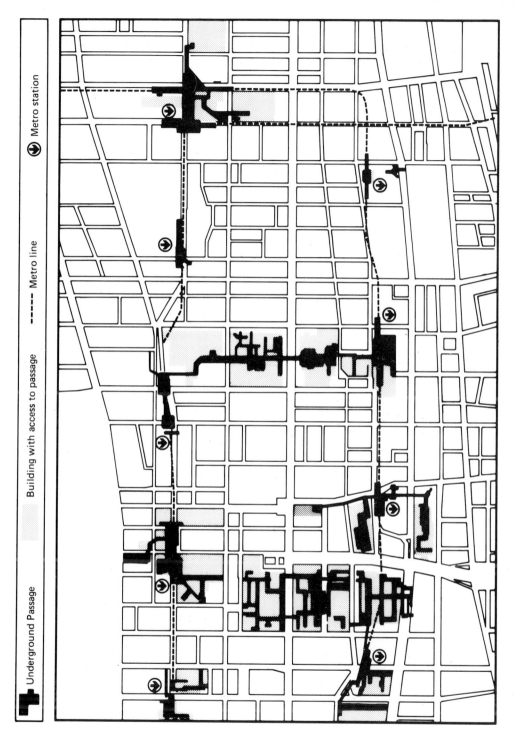

Fig 5.9   Montreal - Underground Connections to Metro

integration attracts much higher office rents. A major developer quoted a figure of 10-15 per cent for the premium which could currently be charged for a prime office development which was linked directly to the underground city.

5.6 Other cities in Canada

5.6.1 Vancouver, British Columbia

The Vancouver Skytrain system opened in 1986 and comprises one line, 22.5 km of track (1.6 km underground, the rest on the surface or elevated) and 15 stations. The system is a fully automatic light rapid transit and cost C$854 million.

In 1975 Vancouver produced a regional land use plan, which proposed to control growth and limit suburban sprawl. The strategy of this plan was to slow city centre growth by creating regional subcentres with office, retail and high density residential components, linked together and to the city centre by rapid transit.

In 1986 Vancouver opened its Skytrain system from downtown Vancouver to New Westminster in order to link the two sites of the EXPO '86 festival, which were at opposite ends of the city. Officials hoped that the line would become Vancouver's growth spine and lifeline between town centres. Patronage rates between January and April were 70,000 journeys per day, equivalent to an annual rate of 26 million journeys per year. During EXPO '86, patronage rose to 150,000 journeys per day. The aggregate patronage figure for 1986 was 35 million journeys.

When the system opened, most of the outlying building activity had focused on the Metrotown station. A one million square foot retail complex was built, along with a corporate headquarters and several office towers. There was also a building boom around several of the stations in downtown Vancouver, especially at the Waterfront station where a world trade centre, convention complex, international pavilion and 700,000 square feet of office space were built.

No parking was provided at any of the stations as land around the stations in built up areas had been increasing in cost. Parking was not seen as an economic use of this land and would have added to the project costs and possibly deterred development.

BC Transit, the regional transit authority, created a property development division which negotiated joint development projects with private interests. These projects were around transit stations; this benefited developers by delivering customers directly to their sites, while offering cash returns and potentially higher ridership to Vancouver's transit authority.

The metro is being extended to Surrey, scheduled to open in February 1990. A further extension to Coquitlam is being planned.

Ambitious zoning for high rise and mixed uses around most stations and the creation of BC Transit's property development division has without question bolstered Vancouver's transit and land use connection.

6 Rapid transit systems in other parts of the world

6.1 Federal Republic of Germany

6.1.1 Hamburg

Hamburg is the model city in West Germany for a fully integrated transport system. The Hamburg Transport Community is the main body that runs the public transport network; it is involved in research, advertising, maintenance, provision of timetables and other public service information.

There are thirteen rapid transit lines, both surface and underground, designed to provide access to densely populated housing belts. 53 per cent of the population uses the rapid transit system. There is a dense bus feeder network to the rapid transit lines, road traffic in the city is kept to a minimum and there are park-and-ride facilities at many of the stations. There is through ticketing, and tickets are interchangeable for different modes of transport. 60 per cent of costs are covered by fare revenue.

The Hamburg area has had a declining population since 1966 and unemployment is higher than average. Growth of the town has mainly been ribbon development, concentrated along the axes of road and rail.

The development of Hamburg has been greatly influenced by the Hamburg density model, especially the planning and the location of housing, and the traffic structure. Heavy capital investment has allowed public transport to compete successfully with the private car in the inner city, in spite of a rise in car ownership and a decentralisation of housing.

The rapid transit system, which is now twenty years old, seems to have encouraged outward movement from the city centre leading to a reduction in population in a zone 5km from the city centre. As the population further out is concentrated along the axes of the rapid transit, it appears that transit has had the effect of enhancing the replacement of residential land uses by work places close to the city centre.

Six km north of the city, and only 2.5 km from the Hamburg-Fuhlsbuttle airport, is City Nord, an office park developed in the mid 1960s, along one of the development axes identified in the density model. By 1980 it comprised 700,000 square metres of office space (compared with 1,860,000 in the city centre), and by 1985 it had 35,000 workers. There was a policy of relocating many office jobs which did not need a city centre location to the fringe of the city centre, so reducing demand for city centre transport. City Nord includes a busy U-Bahn station.

It can be concluded that in Hamburg the recent development of the city was influenced mainly by the Hamburg Density Model rather than the introduction of the rapid transit system, although the ribbon-like development along the rail axes appears to be a result of the rapid transit system.

6.1.2   Hanover

A Transport Authority similar to that in Hamburg was formed in 1970 to provide transport for the city of Hanover and its administrative hinterland. The decision to build an underground tram network was taken in 1965 with the object of avoiding traffic congestion problems in the city centre. The plan was to convert the city gradually to a light rail transit system by putting sections of the existing street tramway underground, but retaining links with the street networks in the suburbs.

In the city centre the system is completely underground, with 12 km of track in tunnel; outside, the system uses separate rights of way (36 km), and shared rights of way (14 km). In the tunnelled sections there are between 35-45 trains an hour, operating automatically, whereas above ground the system uses a mix of visual and automated signals. In the centre of Hanover all stations can be reached within 5 minutes walking time.

In Hanover there was a study aimed at analysing the effect on the city of the first rapid transit network, as an aid to a government cost-benefit analysis of other major transport projects. The study looked at the city centre, two inner city areas and areas around two peripheral interchanges. The study established no connection between the decisions of department stores to settle in the city centre and the completion of line A. However at the time of completion of line A (early 1970s), there was in any case a general acceleration in investment around the main stations, especially the terminus, and the city centre. Though some of this investment was public (eg extensions to the main station, a post office), a lot of the investment was private; for example, the Lister Meille high quality shopping centre, in the area along the new line, had increased its retail floor space.

It is worth noting that at the time the rapid transit was completed there was an extensive redevelopment programme of major parts of the city.

6.1.3   Munich

Munich has an exceptionally good public transport system. In 1937 the council of Munich decided to build an east-west, north-south orientated rail system, but the building of the underground was halted in 1941 due to the war. In 1963 the city council agreed to a general transportation plan which included S-bahn, U-bahn and a tramway system. To provide connections between these systems a tunnel was planned running east-west, crossing the north-south lines, thus providing a vital link between the systems. Construction started in 1965 and finished in 1972 in time for the Olympic Games.

Between the 1950s and 1970s the town grew rapidly; the growth of the town was along the main axes of the rapid transit system. The spatial segregation between home and work grew: in the poorer fringe areas of the city centre lived people who worked in the factories, which were located in the suburbs, and in the richer suburbs lived people who worked in the city. Later development took place further away from the rapid transit system, so these people returned to the car for their transport; this however made the roads congested again. In summary, the effects on the town of the rapid transit system were the separation of population, the segregation of functions, the centralisation of services and retail activities and increase of problems with the new traffic flows.

6.1.4   Rhine-Ruhr

The Rhine-Ruhr region of Germany is a densely populated area with very large industrial sites. The main cities in the region are Dortmund, Essen, Dusseldorf, Duisberg and Bochum. The whole transportation area of the Rhine-Ruhr includes 55 cities, 4 of which have a population over 500,000.

The decision to develop rapid transit was taken in 1974. The Land Government of Nordrhein Westfalen passed legislation to support and finance both a rapid transit system and a regional S-bahn network. The transport authority for the area, the Rhine-Ruhr Light Rail Association, aims to co-ordinate rapid transit in the different cities according to uniform technical standards to give an eventual total planned network of 300 km.

The rapid transit line in Bochum opened in 1975, with extensions in 1986. Dusseldorf opened in 1981 with only two stops on a 1.6 km line; further stretches were opened in 1984. In Essen one line was opened in 1977 from the city centre to Mulham, and later a line from the south west of the city to the university in 1981. The length of the lines within Essen is 10 km and outside the city 5.6 km. Dortmund opened its line in 1984. The whole system is integrated; it is possible to buy one through ticket to use on S-bahn, trams, rapid transit, monorail and trolley-buses.

At the time of building the rapid transit system (1978) there was rapid growth in the area; for example, on one section of the line where one station was planned to be built at a later date (Schiwelm West), there had to be a reappraisal of plans to bring forward its construction date to integrate it with the building of the other twelve stations.

At Dusseldorf's main station the whole area was remodelled as, on the south side, a shopping centre was being established. Another shopping centre (Porsheplatz) was also constructed in Essen above the rapid transit station.

6.1.5   Nuremberg

This is an area similar to the Rhine-Ruhr region as it includes some small cities: Nuremberg itself, Erlangen, Schwabach, Stien and a new town, Langwesser. In 1960 plans were made for an underground system to link the new town to Nuremberg. Building started on this in 1965.

The Sudstadt is an inner city area of Nuremberg just south of the city centre. Before the underground system was developed it had always been an important interchange point for the trams to the city centre, and because of this the Sudstadt was also a shopping area. The new underground system was being built in stages from Langwesser, a satellite town, to the centre of Nuremberg. It was noticed that when the underground reached the Sudstadt there was a boom in the area; shop rents around the station rose and their turnover was higher than those of shops further away. However this 'boom' ended when the underground reached the centre of Nuremberg three years later. Then there was a rapid decline of the Sudstadt; rents and turnovers fell to levels below those of three years before. This decline was blamed on three causes; firstly on the underground itself because shoppers could travel to the city centre without having to change at Sudstadt, but also on the redevelopment and general improvements of Nuremberg's centre which attracted people away from the Sudstadt, and on a shopping centre which was built close to the station shops, having the effect of harming their trade.

6.2   Australia

6.2.1   Sydney

The Sydney monorail opened in 1988 and has a circular track 3.6 km long. The system was built to connect the Darling harbour area to Sydney's extensive suburban rail and bus network. Darling harbour was the site of the largest urban renewal project ever undertaken in Australia. It covered 50 hectares of run-down industrial land, harbour and rail yards, and was converted into a vital new entertainment, cultural, and activity centre. Its features include a convention centre, casino, maritime museum and entertainment centre. Darling harbour was adjacent to an already congested city and needed to be connected to the public transport network to achieve its potential.

6.3   Development impacts in developing countries

A study of Mass Rapid Transit in Developing Countries was carried out by Halcrow Fox and Associates for the Overseas Unit of TRRL, and was reported in June 1989. The study covered 21 cities, including nine with established Metros (Hong Kong, Manila, Mexico City, Porto Alegre, Pusan, Rio de Janeiro, Santiago, Sao Paulo and Seoul) and four with incomplete but recently opened Metros (Cairo, Calcutta, Singapore and Tunis).

The study concluded that in most cities the objectives of increasing the capacity of public transport and the quality of service were both dramatically achieved. As a result, the middle and low income masses were saved a great deal of travel time and discomfort, and the growth of activity in the city centre was able to continue unchecked by declining accessibility. However, in none of the cities studied was a reduction in traffic congestion a notable result. Consequently there was little impact on the environment.

As with countries in the developed world, in the majority of cases the impacts on urban development were small. In Rio, a 1987 study of development impacts of two new lines opened in 1979 and 1981 concluded that no significant impacts resulted. Development in Mexico City occurred away from the rapid transit system, though linked to it by feeder buses. It is therefore difficult to quantify the system's influence. However, assessing development is difficult because many schemes are in their infancy. Those schemes where development occurred generally experienced positive government intervention.

There were a number of examples where developments did occur in conjunction with rapid transit systems. In Santiago (Chile) development occurred at terminus points and in Seoul (Korea) pedestrian shopping centres were integrated with the Metro. In Sao Paulo (Brazil) the government attempted to improve the Metro's catchment area by building low-income housing for 200,000 people near the east line. In Hong Kong development such as 31,000 flats, 435,000 square metres of commercial and industrial space and 140,000 square metres of community space were evidenced in 1986 around the Metro. This development was primarily the result of major government intervention. In both Tunis (Tunisia) and Porto Alegre (Brazil) land prices increased near stations and business development was evident.

On development, the study concluded that

"...In Sao Paulo, Hong Kong and Singapore Metro development has been fully and successfully integrated with major public sector-led development... The Metros have been an important impetus to changing the urban structure. In all other cities the development impact was small, and where there was an identified impact it was difficult to anticipate in advance.

"The growth of the city centre, especially for employment..., could not have taken place without the Metro. This is the major development impact of Metros in developing countries... But the Metro permits, rather than promotes, development and in many cases no impact is discernible. Development requires advance planning if it is to occur quickly and effectively; ...it may not occur spontaneously."

H

7 The effects of rapid transit on patronage and activities

7.1 The effects on public transport patronage

7.1.1 France

Before the opening of rapid transit systems in Lille, Lyon, Marseille and Nantes, the average growth of public transport patronage was about 1 per cent per year (see Table 4). This is the same as the average growth in those cities without a rapid transit system, such as Bordeaux and Toulouse.

Once the rapid transit systems opened the average growth in patronage on all public transport rose to 3.5 per cent per annum, with the patronage on the system itself growing by an average of 10.5 per cent per annum (see Figure 7.1). Some of this growth can be attributed to the opening of additional lines at a later date. Another reason for the growth is that the figures in Table 4 are calculated from passenger boardings. When a rapid transit system is introduced, passenger boardings can increase, even if the number of passenger trips do not. This due to passengers having to interchange between bus and the rapid transit system, where before a single bus journey would get them to their destination.

After 7 or 8 years, the metros in Marseille, Lyon and Lille had increased total public transport journeys by 30 per cent, 21 per cent and 58 per cent respectively. In Nantes, passenger journeys increased by 28 per cent between 1984 and 1988, and in Grenoble an increase of around 15 per cent was found.

The figures used below are mainly from surveys carried out on the metro systems of Lille, Lyon and Marseille.

TABLE 4
ANNUAL GROWTH OF PUBLIC TRANSPORT PATRONAGE, FRENCH CITIES

	Growth before the Metro	Growth after the Metro	Growth of the Metro
Lille	0.25%	4.0%	11.0%
Lyon*	2.3%	3.0%	7.0%
Marseille*	-3.5%	3.0%	14.0%
Nantes	4.8%	4.0%	10.0%
Bordeaux	1.0%		
Strasbourg	0.2%		
Toulouse	1.5%		

* All data are from 1980 to 1987 except Lyon and Marseille which are from 1975 to 1987

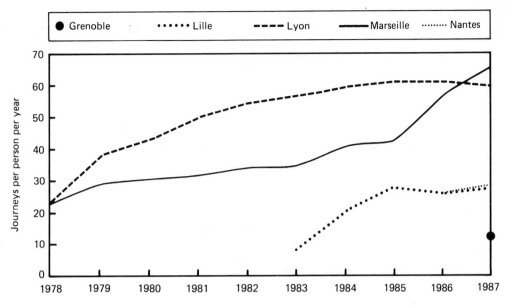

Fig 7.1   French rapid transit systems: Patronage

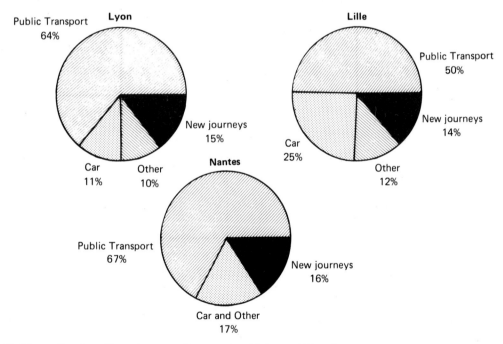

Fig 7.2   French rapid transit systems: Passenger travel before rapid transit

Before the rapid transit systems opened between 50 per cent (in Lille) and 67 per cent (in Nantes) of the passengers used to use some other form of public transport to make their journeys (as shown in Figure 7.2). Around 15 per cent of the trips on the rapid transit system are trips which were not made previously. Ex-car users account for around 12 per cent of the rapid transit passengers, except in Lille where 25 per cent used to use the car. By comparison, in Tyne and Wear, an area of low car ownership, 8 per cent of Metro travellers used to go by car. The higher proportion in Lille is believed to be because the corridor between Lille and Villeneuve d'Ascq was poorly served by buses before.

The conclusion would seem to be that rapid transit is attractive to car travellers, whether by virtue of its speed advantage over buses, more comfortable journey, or better image. While the corresponding reduction in road traffic is barely noticeable, it is possible that it is sufficient to allow the introduction of traffic restraint measures such as pedestrianisation. The converse is also possible: that the reduction in road capacity which pedestrianisation causes induces some car travellers to switch to public transport. In all the French cities, pedestrianisation of part of the city centre was carried out at about the same time as the rapid transit line was introduced or soon afterwards, so it is not possible to distinguish which is cause and effect, though in Marseille and Lille the schemes were not extensive and probably had little effect on road traffic, while Grenoble is small enough for most central areas to be accessible by car anyway. However, it is the opinion in more than one city that installing an alternative form of public transport makes it more acceptable to introduce measures such as pedestrianisation which have a restraining effect on traffic.

Users of the rapid transit are split evenly by sex. Compared with British bus passengers, 60 per cent of whom are women, more men use the French rapid transit systems. 60 per cent of the passengers use rapid transit once or more a day. Around a quarter of passengers use it several times a week and only 15 per cent use it occasionally.

One of the main uses of rapid transit is for trips to and from work which account for 37 per cent of journeys (see Figure 7.3). Around 18 per cent of journeys are to and from school, while 10 per cent are shopping trips. The remaining 35 per cent of the journeys are either other reasons or are secondary trips. The picture is different in Lille, where the Metro serves the large university in Villeneuve d'Ascq. Trips to school and university form 34 per cent of the total, while work trips are only 21 per cent. The proportions of trips made for shopping, secondary and other purposes are about the same as in other French cities, implying that students make these trips as often as the general population.

In Lille over half (54 per cent) of the people who use the Metro are students (or school pupils). This compares with 27 per cent in the other French cities (as shown in Figure 7.4). Those with no full time job, such as the unemployed and retired, make up 14 per cent of the passengers. The rest are those in full time employment and comprise about 58 per cent, except in Lille where they only make up 34 per cent because many students use the system.

Most of the people who use rapid transit get to the system on foot (64 per cent; in Lille 74 per cent). In all three French cities the car is used by about 4 per cent to get to the rapid transit, while the bus is used by 28 per cent (except in Lille, where only 14 per cent use it).

7.1.2   USA

The figures used below are from surveys carried out in Atlanta, San Diego and San Francisco.

In San Diego the average annual growth in public transport patronage is 7.3 per cent, since its

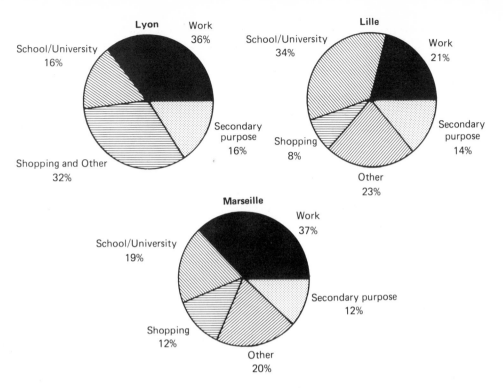

Fig 7.3   French rapid transit systems: Reasons for using rapid transit

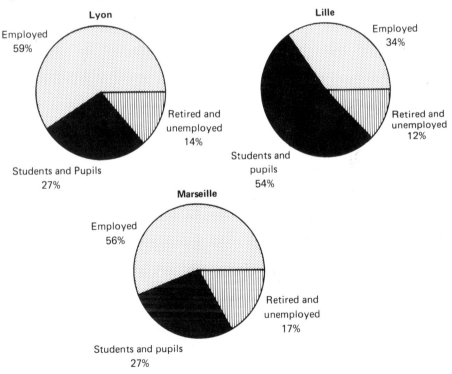

Fig 7.4   French rapid transit systems: Users of rapid transit

111

rapid transit system opened. This growth is especially significant when compared with a 6 per cent drop in patronage in areas not served by the rapid system in the same period. In San Francisco (BART) patronage grew on average, by about 5 per cent a year in the first 12 years of operation.

In San Diego 10 per cent of the trips on the trolley system are new trips generated by the introduction of the system. 56.4 per cent of the passengers used to travel by bus and 29.8 per cent used to use a car.

In Atlanta users of Metro are split evenly by sex, but in San Diego considerably more men (61 per cent) than women use the rapid transit system. This may be due to the large number of military personnel living and working in the area and to Mexican workers travelling to the city from the border. In both cities about 2 per cent of the passengers are under 16, but more old people ride the system in San Diego, where 10 per cent of the passengers are 60 and over, and only 49 per cent fall into the 25 to 59 age range, than in Atlanta, where only 3 per cent are 60 and over and 63 per cent of the passengers are aged between 25 and 59.

In San Diego the less well off with incomes of less than $5,000 comprise 15 per cent of the rapid transit passengers (probably the Mexican workers again), while in Atlanta they only make up 10 per cent of the passengers. A large percentage of passengers on rapid transit do not have a private vehicle available as an alternative means of making the journey. In Atlanta the figure is 70 per cent, in San Diego 60 per cent and in San Francisco 56 per cent.

In both San Francisco and Atlanta, over 60 per cent of the journeys made on rapid transit are journeys to and from work. Of the remainder, in both cities around 12 per cent are school trips and 14 per cent are for personal business.

In San Diego over half (58 per cent) of the rapid transit passengers walk to the system, 22 per cent use a car and 20 per cent use the bus. In Atlanta, the most popular way of reaching the Metro is by bus (42 per cent); only 34 per cent walk and 21 per cent use a car. In San Francisco during peak periods, over half (52 per cent) of the passengers arrive by car, 27 per cent walk and 19 per cent use the buses.

7.1.3   Canada

When Calgary opened its tramway system in 1981, a survey was carried out to assess the impact of the system. Additional surveys were carried out in 1985 and 1987, when new lines were opened. All the surveys were conducted in the morning peak, between 6:00 AM and 9:00 AM.

When the first (southern) line opened in 1981 30 per cent of the passengers on the system were making trips that they did not previously make. But when the second (northeast) line opened in 1985 only 4 per cent of the passengers were making new trips. On the third (northwest) line, the percentage of passengers making new trips was 8 per cent. However on all lines around 16 per cent of passengers used to travel by car and about 3 per cent used some other means of transport, or walked. 49 per cent of passengers on the southern line, 79 per cent of northeastern line passengers and 74 per cent of passengers on the northwestern line used to travel by bus.

As can be expected, most of the trips on all lines in the peak period are to work: 93 per cent southern line, 95 per cent northeastern line and 87 per cent on the northwestern line. School trips make up 6 per cent of southern line trips, 11 per cent of northwestern line trips and only 3 per cent of northeastern line trips. The low percentage of school trips on the Northeastern line is due to the time of year that the survey was carried out. Not surprisingly, less than 1 per cent of peak hour trips were for shopping. However a second survey carried out during off-peak hours on the southern line shows that 21 per cent of off peak trips are for shopping, 30 per cent for work and 15 per cent are school trips. The results from a survey in Edmonton are 52 per cent work trips, 21 per cent school and university trips and 27 per cent shopping and other purposes.

On the northeastern and northwestern lines in Calgary about 74 per cent of the passengers had a car available to make the trip. On these two lines a large proportion of the passengers (about 68 per cent) made 6 to 10 trips on the system each week, 26 per cent of users travelled 1 to 5 times a week and 6 per cent made 11 to 15 trips. Less than 1 per cent of the passengers made 16 or more trips a week. On all three lines about half of the passengers arrived at the stations by bus. On the southern and northeastern lines about 35 per cent of passengers came by car and 15 per cent walked to the station. However on the northwestern line only 17 per cent of passengers arrived by car. This is because only one of the stations on the northwestern line has park-and-ride facilities. The survey in Edmonton revealed that 33 per cent of passengers arrived at the station by bus, 63 per cent walk to the station and 4 per cent arrived by car.

7.1.4   Germany

In Germany, Hall and Hass-Klau (1985) concluded that rail investments "strikingly halted or even reversed" the decline in public transport patronage. In Munich, Hanover and Nuremberg, patronage grew at 2 to 3 per cent per annum where it was stable before, in Cologne a decline of 1 per cent per annum was halted, and in Essen a decline of 2 per cent per annum became a growth of 1 per cent. By contrast, two German cities which did not invest in urban rail (Dortmund and Bremen) had fairly stable patronage over a similar period.

7.2   The effects on activities

7.2.1   Shopping

In France, only about 10 per cent of the journeys on the rapid transit systems are for shopping. Over half of the shopping trips take place between two and six in the afternoon. There is some evidence for an increase in shopping, especially in the central areas, in a few cities. In Grenoble and Nantes, a number of new shops have opened since the tramways were put into service. In Lyon, there has been an increase in shopping activity, at the expense, it is claimed, of shops in the inner suburbs. The city centre of Lyon has extended, though this is partly due to the development at Part Dieu, which was unconnected with the Metro. As far as other countries are concerned, there is very little information available. It is claimed that shopping in the centre of Washington has been rejuvenated by the Metro, and there were new shopping centres in some of the cities in Germany.

These results can be compared with a study in Newcastle, where activity in the city centre was strengthened by the Tyne and Wear Metro. Many shop managers in Newcastle and other centres believed the Metro helped to increase their trade. Increased development interest and retail levels in certain locations reflected the Metro's existence.

7.2.2 Employment

Employment opportunities resulting from the development of a rapid transit system can be classified into those related to the construction and operation of the system and those related to increased accessibility and development potential.

The Washington Metro employs 2,163 staff, the Boston rapid transit 711 and the Lille Metro 185. The lower numbers of staff on the Lille Metro result from the unmanned VAL system. Therefore the technology employed (affecting levels of research and development), together with the physical size, management capacities and levels of subsidies provided, affects employment levels with regard to systems operation. Construction of a metro system also employs substantial numbers of people.

The extent to which a rapid transit system can directly influence employment is difficult to quantify. The question is whether these opportunities would have resulted if the system was not developed at all, and whether new jobs are created or are redistributed from other areas, thereby not increasing the overall level of employment opportunities.

Detailed studies are required in order to identify the effects of rapid transit on employment, probably involving questionnaire surveys of employees, and few such studies are available. Some results are given below.

In Washington, a survey was carried out for Metropolitan Washington Council of Governments (MWCOG 1980, 1985), which studied employment change in Metrorail station areas. The indications were contrary to expectation. The survey found that while total employment in the region grew by 15 per cent in this period, employment in the Metrorail station areas grew by less than 7 per cent, compared to an increase of 26 per cent in other areas. 52 per cent of the jobs in the region in 1985 were located in Metrorail station areas, a 4 per cent decline from 1980. This probably had more to do with growth in higher-income employment, where people choose to live in pleasant low-density suburban areas, rather than with the Metro itself.

The Washington Post (1984) reported the failure of Metro to attract large scale employment and commented that Metro's role in economic development remained questionable. Population was now more dispersed along the line and only a small proportion used Metro.

A study in San Francisco (U.S. Department of Transportation and U.S. Department of Housing and Urban Development (1979)) concluded that there were 1265 permanent additional jobs in the Bay Area as a direct result of BART operations compared with the No-BART Alternative. Many of the impacts of BART were short term impacts of construction and did not amount in any one year to more than one half of one percent of the total regional employment. Thus the Economics and Finance Project concluded that the regional economic impacts did not have a 'significant long term impact' on the total regional economy (McDonald & Grefe Inc, 1978).

In Atlanta, an employment analysis was carried out as part of the TIMP (Transit Impact Monitoring Study). However, no causative relationship could be found which would tie significant employment growth or decline to proximity to the system. Employment change in the station areas was found to have been influenced more by the prevailing national and regional economic conditions of the period.

In Marseille Simpson (1989) concluded that the Metro served areas which were mainly dependent on central area employment instead of the working class districts to the north and east. Thus it helped to maintain activities in the city centre and accentuate the distinction between employment in the centre and residence in the suburbs.

In Tyne and Wear integration of the public transport system made journeys to work easier and faster but was not found to increase employment levels and there was no evidence of any significant change in the catchment areas of employment centres within the older industrial areas. Questionnaire surveys in 1980 and 1983 (MMDS 1985), when most of Metro was in operation, showed that in both years about 35 per cent of journeys to workplaces were made by public transport, though in 1983 the decline in employment levels had reduced the total number of journeys. However, people making new journeys to work were more likely to use the Metro than the bus (Tyne and Wear County Council et al).

The development of the London Docklands Light Railway has been partly responsible for various new employment opportunities relating to offices, shops and housing. In 1986 it was forecast that 90,000 extra jobs would be created. In 1985 92,000 sq. ft. of office floor space was completed and an estimated 2.7m sq. ft. will be completed by 1990. From 1990 onwards forecasts of an additional 23.9m sq. ft. of office space have been made. It has been estimated that the Docklands working population will increase from the 1986 figure of 30,500 to 200,000+ by the year 2000.

8 Conclusions from overseas rapid transit systems

In this section we draw together the findings from the study of rapid transit systems in other countries to identify the features which have been important in determining the effects of these systems on transport and urban development in their cities.

The fourteen systems studied in France, the USA and Canada vary considerably in terms of their objectives, costs, patronage and effects. In order to understand the effects of these systems on urban development, it is necessary to view the systems in the widest context. Consequently, we consider first some of the wider aspects before dealing more specifically with the effects on urban development.

8.1 The objectives for rapid transit systems

We have observed a wide range of objectives for developing metro and light rail systems. Although most systems are the result of a combination of several objectives, their relative importance varies considerably.

8.1.1 Transport objectives

The first, and usually the major, objective in the systems examined was to improve public transport - in other words to provide a faster, more reliable, greater capacity transport system than could be provided by buses alone. In order to maximise the benefits from the investment in a rail system, transport services in the city are usually integrated, with feeder buses serving metro or tramway stations, often with a common flat-fare ticketing system.

These transport objectives are often coupled with a desire to provide an alternative to congested roads, and even to reduce congestion itself. Rail systems are also seen as improving business activity, by means of bringing more customers into the city centre, and helping workers to get to work more easily.

The French systems all had improving public transport and reducing congestion as their main objectives, and in Marseille the investment was entirely justified on these grounds. The older systems in Canada (Montreal and Toronto) were justified on the grounds that a rail system was needed to meet the growing demand for public transport. More recently, rapid transit has been seen as a means of reversing the trend towards the car and attracting passengers back to public transport.

Following the experience of rapidly expanding sprawling suburbs which have given rise to severe transport problems, planners in several cities are attempting to focus urban growth in particular areas. Transport links in the form of light rail or metro systems are often seen as the ideal form of transport provision. Examples of this can be found in Lyon and Lille, where the metros were designed to provide links between developing suburbs and the city centre.

8.1.2 Objectives relating to environment and image

Rapid transit is seen as a way of improving the environment, particularly in terms of reducing pollution from cars and (especially in the USA) of reducing the need for highway construction. Environmental pressures in the USA resulted in legislation which permitted states to transfer money allocated to highway schemes into rapid transit schemes. The construction of the tramway in Sacramento was largely made possible through the diversion of highway funds, in the face of opposition from the Federal authorities. The importance of environmental issues on the west coast of the USA is highlighted by a recent decision to set stringent vehicle emission standards in California.

Rapid transit is also seen as a way of improving the image of the city. In part, this is a function of making the city a more attractive place to be, with fast comfortable access, pedestrianised streets, less traffic, shiny modern transport, etc. In part, it is a psychological effect of the city being seen as having confidence in itself. In this way, it is hoped to attract investment and industry to the area. These objectives were particularly important in Calgary and in Grenoble, but were also part of the justification in Lyon and Lille. In the latter case, the Metro was in some respects a demonstration project for the company which developed the automatic system.

8.1.3 Objectives relating to urban form

In some cities rapid transit systems are intended to improve urban structure, by providing opportunities for developments. In the older Canadian systems (Toronto and Montreal) and in Marseille, this objective took the form of allowing the city to expand. In Toronto, the planners are trying to concentrate new growth around particular stations. Focusing growth around the subway avoids the situation which has arisen in Montreal, where many people have chosen to live further out from the city centre, partly because the city taxes are so high. As these areas are not yet served by the subway, this has generated a huge increase in commuter car traffic crossing the bridges onto the main island. One of the prime motives for building metros in developing countries is to enable the planners to focus urban development.

These planning objectives are becoming increasingly important. The new line (Line D) in Lyon and the VAL system in Lille were justified partly on the grounds of improving the urban structure. In Toronto and Edmonton, one of the objectives was to prevent urban sprawl by strengthening the central business district.

The prominent example of development objectives for a rail system is Atlanta, where the Metro was planned from the start as part of an urban development plan, with zones around certain stations earmarked for development.

117

8.1.4   Personal and political objectives

Rapid transit systems currently attract a lot of support from local politicians. This enthusiasm is often much stronger than can be justified by any economic considerations of the systems. For example, the federal agencies in the USA have strict guidelines for assessing the eligibility of schemes for funding. Nevertheless, some of the less successful US rail systems (Sacramento, Miami) were pushed through by Congress in the face of unpromising assessments by UMTA. Moreover, the local enthusiasm does not seem to diminish when the systems subsequently open with comparatively poor financial results.

Although these are not usually quoted as reasons for building a rail system, there is no doubt that a strong personality who can exert influence is sometimes an important factor in the decision. The influence of the Mayors in Nantes and Grenoble has already been noted. Similar personal influences have been found in the United States, where the cities consist of a number of separate municipalities, each with its own set of politicians, and the routeing and design of the transport system is influenced by the lobbying of these local personalities. It may also be significant that the Atlanta Metro project and the growth of Atlanta as a regional centre began at a time when Georgia was the home state of the US President.

8.2   Funding methods

There is a wide variety of methods of funding for rapid transit systems, especially between one country and another and, in the United States, between one State or city and another. They can, however, be classified into three main areas: funding from revenues, funding from taxation by means of grants and subsidies, and funding from the private sector, where contributions from property developers are becoming increasingly important.

8.2.1   Funding from revenues

Most of the systems studied in this report do not cover their operating costs, though some lose less money than others. Typically, the transport network as a whole covers 50-60 per cent of its operating cost from the farebox. The Federal view in the USA is that systems should be more cost effective, but several disastrously uneconomic systems have been approved by Congress (Miami and St Louis for example).

Most cities where figures are available show an increase in the revenue to operating cost ratio following the opening of the rail system, and where there are separate figures for rail these are generally higher than for the public transport network as a whole. It would therefore appear that the rapid transit systems studied are nearer to covering their operating costs than the bus systems which they replace, though they involve greater capital cost.

Almost all the systems studied are integrated with the bus system. This means that it is quite difficult to separate the costs and particularly the revenues for each mode. However, in general, integration with buses improves the revenue to operating cost ratio of the rail mode at the expense of the bus mode. This is because rapid transit systems carry many passengers who transfer from buses, and passengers using several modes usually pay a heavily discounted price for the ticket. Without integration, many of the passengers might choose to use direct bus services.

One or two rail systems come close to covering their operating costs: San Diego (a simple low cost system with a strong tourist traffic) achieves a 90 per cent revenue to operating cost ratio, Lille (where the automatic system allows a drastic reduction in operating cost, albeit at great capital expense) achieves 95 per cent, and in Lyon the Metro system was reported as covering its operating costs and making a contribution towards the subsidy required for the rest of the network.

8.2.2   Funding from taxation sources

It is common for part of the funding for a rapid transit system to come from public funds, in the form of grants towards capital expenditure and/or subsidies towards operating costs. In most cases, local government provides part of the capital cost of the system with the remainder from regional or national government grants. These grants may be made according to a defined assessment process, or with each case being considered on an ad hoc basis.

The transit systems in Alberta (Calgary and Edmonton) make use of provincial grants which may be used to cover 75 per cent of any approved transport infrastructure. Each city receives around C$40 million grant per year. This method of funding has encouraged the harmonisation of highways and rapid transit, such as the development of the rail line along a highway median.

In Sacramento, funds which were allocated for highway use were transferred to rapid transit construction. This produced a surge in rapid transit development, at the expense, naturally, of highway construction.

Rail systems in the USA can also be eligible for Federal grant. The criteria which they have to meet are clearly specified. The process of applying for federal grant can take a long time, and this has been a deterrent for some authorities.

In France, the Government used to provide grants of 50 per cent of the infrastructure cost to worthwhile schemes, though this percentage has been reduced in recent years because of increasing demands on the funds available.

Earmarked taxes, in the form of state or employment taxes designated for use in providing transport, provide predictable funding because they do not rely on allocations from annual budgets. In some countries, where an operating deficit is expected, the availability of assured funding is a very important factor in deciding whether anything will be built. In France, Versement Transport is an employment tax raised directly through the employers. Transport authorities can use employment projections to forecast their future income; there is the added advantage (from the authority's point of view) that the income keeps pace with inflation to the extent that wages do. In San Diego, Sacramento and other US cities, sales taxes and other local taxes are used for funding the construction and operating costs.

8.2.3 Funding from developer contributions

For many rapid transit proposals it is expected that there would be a considerable increase in land values and property prices, particularly near to stations. If some of these increases could be recouped and channelled towards the capital costs of a rapid transit system, they could make a significant contribution. Developers, industrialists and others with an interest in the value of the land may see the development of a rapid transit system as beneficial and they may be willing to make contributions to its funding to ensure that it is built.

In several cities in the USA and Canada, the development of rapid transit has been partly financed by deals between the public authorities and private sector entrepreneurs. However, in none of the systems visited in this study was there a significant contribution to the basic capital costs of the system from the private sector. Examples were found, as in Toronto, where developers had paid for ancillary features such as extensions, the connection of a new development to a station or the provision of road access.

One reason for this is that in the USA it has been found that developers do not want to be urban pioneers; they feel it is too risky to be the first development in the rail corridor, and hesitate about making a commitment to invest without a reasonable probability that the system will be built. Uncertainty hinders planning and increases private sector risk, leading to higher costs. If, on the other hand, developers can have confidence that their contribution to the funding of the system will help to ensure that it is built, they are more likely to be interested in contributing and in pursuing development opportunities.

The time taken to get approval for grants is very important, particularly if private developers are involved, as speculative financial decisions are usually quite short term, and developers get frustrated at the length of time taken to complete all the stages of the planning/consultation process. Several systems in the USA have decided not to go for Federal funding for this reason. An example illustrating this point occurred in New Jersey, where the development of waste land at the Waterfront was planned in connection with a rapid transit line, but delays led to developers losing confidence that the line would ever be built. As a result, they went ahead with an alternative development which was not so well matched to the rail line.

8.2.4 The role of the funding mechanism in promoting confidence

Constructing rapid transit schemes, like any project which requires large capital investment, involves an element of risk. Operators of transport systems, governments who provide grants, and developers who might want to exploit development opportunities or contribute to the funding of the rapid transit line, need to have confidence that the system is a sound proposal which has a realistic possibility of being built and will be adequately funded in the future. The risk is then minimised, and they may be more willing to put funds into the scheme. If, on the other hand, it appears that the scheme will be underfunded or will be an open-ended commitment in the future, then developers and operators are likely to want some other reassurance.

With most rapid transit schemes in other countries, governments and local authorities underwrite the risk by their commitment to public transport. A prime example can be found in Toronto, where a consistent high priority to public transport, backed up by expansion and investment, has produced a very impressive system which has a high level of public confidence and is well used (though placing an increasing strain on the public purse). However, in Montreal, which is otherwise similar, the gradually increasing involvement of the Province in subway development has resulted in reviews, changes of plans and a slowing down of construction. The general lower level of confidence by developers in Montreal may be attributed in part to this uncertainty.

In the case of capital costs, some governments provide grants according to criteria which are, to a greater or lesser extent, pre-defined, so that promoters can form a realistic assessment of whether their scheme is likely to qualify. In the case of operating costs, the provision of subsidies or income from local taxes lessens the risk that the scheme will not have adequate funds available.

Where operators and developers can see that grants are available towards the capital cost, and that subsidies can offset the risk of an operating loss, they can be more confident that the scheme is a realistic possibility and will be more willing to invest their own funds. This also makes it easier to obtain loans to cover the remainder of the costs.

The consistency of policies favouring public transport and availability of grants and subsidies would appear to be significant reasons why the development of rapid transit systems in other countries has proceeded so rapidly in recent years. However, funding from taxation also has important disadvantages. If grants for construction are too readily available, developers may lack any incentive to contribute to the scheme at all, unless the commitment to building the system is made subject to a successful outcome of negotiations between the proposer and property developers. Transport authorities may also be tempted to become overcommitted on the basis of future income which later proves to be insufficient.

Local taxes such as sales or payroll taxes may cause movements in residence, place of work or shopping to neighbouring authorities in the suburbs, distorting travel patterns and increasing mileage. Operating subsidies can lead to inefficiency, by reducing the incentive to control costs and improve productivity and by "leakage" into high wages and expansion of services. This is especially true of earmarked taxes, which reduce accountability to voters and the need to justify expenditure. The question of whether the funds could be better used - in the transport sector or outside - may not be addressed.

The question of where the funding for a new system comes from has a substantial effect on the implementation. Where cities fund the rail system locally, there are likely to be wider effects as the system is more closely related to the planning aims. The prominent example of this is in Atlanta, where the Metro was planned as an integral part of the development plans for the city. The organisation of the whole planning process was reoriented around the rapid transit system. By contrast, the Baltimore system was mainly State and Federally funded, and the transport authority had little involvement with planning decisions. In this case, planning decisions can even be in conflict with the transit authority, for example, on car parking policy.

8.3　Rapid transit and patronage

There is a very wide range of patronage among the rail systems studied. Figure 8.1 shows the patronage per kilometre of line for each of the cities covered in this report, with the addition of the Tyne and Wear Metro for comparison purposes. It can be seen that the busiest system (Lyon) has over 10 times the patronage of the least (San Diego). There can be a number of reasons for these variations; obviously the local features in each area (eg fares, population, level of employment) will affect the patronage greatly, but some themes can be discerned, as noted in the following paragraphs.

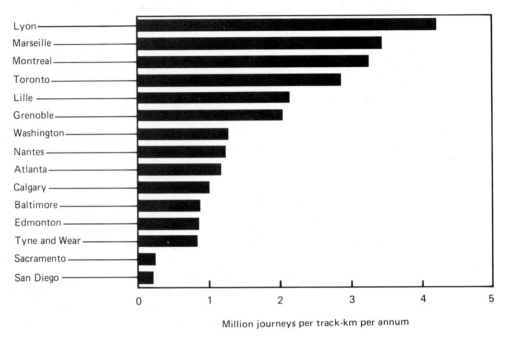

Million journeys per track-km per annum

Fig 8.1　Rapid transit systems: Journeys per kilometre

8.3.1　Urban form

The actual form of the cities has an effect on the patronage. In the French cities and in Toronto, land use densities are high. This favours public transport; more people live within walking distance of a station and the city itself tends to be more compact so that a given length of line serves a higher population. Road traffic tends to be more congested which also favours a rail mode. Sacramento, by contrast, has a low density of population, and the correspondingly lower patronage per kilometre reflects this.

In cities with high land use densities, not only do more people live close to the line, but they also have different life styles which are more likely to involve travel in the evenings. City centres thronging with life and people sitting in street cafes are common in France and are partly a result of living in high rise apartments without gardens.

The mixture of land uses can also have a marked effect on the use made of a rail system. For example, Toronto is a well-established city with a traditional centre offering a wide range of shops and leisure facilities which are open well into the evening; as a result, the streets are crowded late at night and the Metro is extensively used for long periods of the day. Washington, on the other hand, is a city of office workers and the centre is very quiet at night. If a Metro system is little used at night it can become an undesirable place to be, which can itself further discourage patronage; Marseille also tends to suffer in this respect.

8.3.2   Features of existing transport

Obviously, the patronage on a new metro or light rail system is dependent on the remainder of the transport system. In the USA, public transport usage tends to be low, and in some of the smaller cities such as Sacramento or San Diego can be as low as 3-4 per cent of journeys. In circumstances where most people have made other arrangements for their journeys, it is unrealistic to expect a rail system to make much impact.

This problem is compounded by the fact that in many US cities access by car is good. In San Diego, in Calgary and in Baltimore, for example, the tramway runs alongside a major highway, which may reduce the impact since it would then lose much of its speed advantage over car, though this could be outweighed by better access in the city centre.

8.3.3   Features of the rail system

Equally obviously, the patronage on a new rail system depends on what facilities that system offers to the passenger. The first feature to consider is the size of the system as compared with the size of the city. When a metro or tramway is introduced, it is generally a short stretch of the most profitable line which is built first - usually from the city centre along a major radial. As the system is extended out into the suburbs, it reaches areas where the population density is much lower or even which are not yet built up. The patronage per kilometre of track is bound to be lower in such circumstances. The system in Washington, for example, is very extensive, covering over 70 miles; many parts of the system are therefore likely to be lightly used. The Tyne and Wear Metro and the Baltimore system also cover low density suburban areas.

By contrast, the Metro in Lyon and the tramway in Grenoble extend only as far as the edge of the highly-trafficked area, relying on feeder buses to serve the suburbs; their patronage is correspondingly higher. But this process can perhaps be carried too far; the Edmonton tramway covers only a small portion of the city with 8 stations, and in these circumstances it is hardly worth the passenger's while to change from a feeder bus. This is reflected in Edmonton's low patronage figure.

The bus network itself will have an effect on rail patronage. If there is an extensive feeder network bringing in passengers from all areas, then clearly the patronage on the rail system will be higher. An integrated network, with through tickets and well connected interchange, will also increase rail patronage.

A negative example of the effect of feeder buses is provided by Grenoble where, although like Toronto the streets are busy at night, people tend not to use the tramway for their visits. The reason (apart from the fact that access by car is relatively easy) is that although the tram runs until after midnight, the feeder buses stop at 9:30; clearly, no-one is going to use the tramway if they cannot get home again.

In some cities, for example Toronto, Montreal and Grenoble, the rail system has been integrated with the destinations as well, by allowing access from stations direct into shopping centres and offices.

In some cases there are special features which affect patronage. A case in point is San Diego, where the trolley line runs to the nearby Mexican border. This has two effects. One is that the border itself is an attraction and many tourists use the trolley to visit it. The other is that many of the large number of Mexicans employed in the city and dockyards in San Diego make the daily journey to and from the border by trolley.

8.3.4   Changes in patronage

In cities or countries with a tradition of high public transport use, new rail systems will be well used. In nearly all of the cities studied, public transport patronage has increased, not only when the system was first introduced, but for a number of years afterwards. In some cases, Marseille for instance, this increase has been very substantial. Around half to two-thirds of the passengers on the new rapid transit system previously used another means of public transport, but half the remainder are former car users and the other half are making trips which were not previously made. The effect on car traffic, though, is not noticeable, and in cities where public transport use is low, rail may attract a few car users but will not make a dramatic impact.

There is thus some evidence that the steady decline in public transport use which is found in many cities can be retarded, or even reversed, by investment in rapid transit systems. Rail systems - especially light rail or modern tramway systems - have a number of advantages over buses, in that they have generally higher average speeds, smoother acceleration, and better penetration of pedestrianised areas of the city. Rail systems also appear to have a better image than buses and attract more passengers who are likely to have a car alternative.

8.4   Traffic, environment and image

In many European cities, it has been found that rapid transit can make the city centre more attractive, if the centre is pedestrianised so that people can walk about unhindered by traffic. This has occurred in Lyon, Grenoble, Nantes, and to a small extent in Lille, as well as in some German cities. The tramway in Sacramento was also installed with such enhancement of the city centre in mind. In Marseille, by contrast, the pedestrianisation is limited to one main shopping street, and the Metro has had little effect on the attractiveness of the city centre.

City authorities claim that they have been able to pedestrianise their city centres because of the reduction in traffic caused by the Metro or tramway. Since many rail users are former car users, one would expect some reduction in traffic, in the absence of suppressed demand. In Lille, it is estimated that 3000 car trips per day were transferred to rail in the city centre, but the noticeable effect on congestion is minimal, because it would appear that the reduction in traffic was taken up by car journeys which would not have otherwise been made.

However, installing rapid transit can make it more acceptable to introduce traffic restraint measures such as parking and pedestrianisation, as in Munich, Lyon and Grenoble. The reduction in traffic caused by such measures, rather than by any voluntary transfer of car users to public transport, is likely to be the major effect. The resulting disbenefits to car users must be set against the environmental benefits obtained.

As some of the systems are being extended into residential areas, the residents are often more concerned about attracting undesirable people out from the city than with the benefits to be derived from the greater accessibility. This effect was noticed in Montreal, and in Nantes an attitude survey found that residents had noticed "the trams full of young unemployed people."

Rapid transit is thought to improve the image of the city itself and to help in attracting investment to the area. Developers in Nantes thought that the tramway was a good thing and that it improved the image of the town, as well as being a development factor. "Improved civic pride" was felt to be a result in Marseille. In Calgary a survey of business owners and operators (City of Calgary 1989) carried out in September 1986, during the NWLRT construction period, found that 55 per cent of respondents thought their business would improve. There is, though, scanty evidence for any real effects in terms of, for example, companies moving into the area, and there are usually other factors involved, for example the coming of the TGV in Grenoble.

8.5   Development and land use

8.5.1   Most development effects are long-term

There can be no doubt that, in the long term - after fifty or a hundred years - urban rail systems have a profound effect on urban development; large cities like London and Paris would not have developed in the way they have without their Metro and suburban rail systems. The effect of urban rail on the shape of the city over twenty years or so is also clearly visible in cities where Metros were introduced in the Sixties; the newer areas of Toronto, Montreal and Hamburg cited in this report are evidence of this.

Experience from developing countries suggests that cities such as Mexico City which are growing rapidly reach a point - at a population of 1 or 2 million - where they cannot grow any more without a rapid transit system; the number of people employed in the city centre simply exceeds the capacity of the road system to bring them to work. Without a transit system, the city must either stop growing or develop into a polycentric city. In Mexico City and other similar expanding cities, then, rapid transit has allowed a natural growth to continue, and over the longer term the cities will probably show obvious signs of development along the transit corridors as London and Paris do now.

I*

In this report we are more concerned with shorter-term developments in urban form - within 5 or 10 years of the opening of a rail system. This is because the possibility of urban development resulting from investment in rapid transit in British cities can be a factor which helps to decide whether that rail system will be built. There is a possibility that developers might be willing to contribute to the cost of the system, or that development benefits (whether recouped from the developers or not) can be taken into account in deciding whether the system should qualify for grant.

It should be stated, however, that in most cases promoting urban development is not the primary aim of building a rapid transit system. Most rail systems studied in this report were built to transport people, not to promote development. In some cases where tramways have been introduced with environmental objectives, such as in Edmonton and Sacramento, there have actually been restraints on additional development. Even in Atlanta, where the Metro was planned as an integral part of the land use plan, in some areas there was a positive attempt to discourage development.

8.5.2   The importance of planning

The systems where the greatest effect on urban development has occurred are those where there has been a long process of urban planning in conjunction with the rail system. This has resulted in a symbiotic integration of transport and land use: the new transport system provides the opportunities for land development, which in turn generates demand for travel, and leads to the success of an area generally. The prime example of this is in Atlanta, but similar effects can be seen in Washington, Montreal and Toronto where office and shopping developments are linked into Metro stations, and in Hamburg, Hanover and Munich where extensive city centre redevelopments were undertaken at the same time as the rail lines were introduced.

Even without this history of strategic planning, many of the most impressive examples of urban development occur where central planning is used to integrate development with a new line. Examples of this are the La Rose development in Marseille, the planning of the Metro to link Lille with the new town of Villeneuve d'Ascq, and the use of height restrictions in Grenoble and monetary incentives in Sacramento to favour development in the rail corridor. Even in Baltimore, one of the least successful systems in terms of promoting development, the introduction of the Metro was connected with the development of the downtown area with Federal funds.

Developers have usually been encouraged to locate in the areas around stations by means of incentives and discouraged from locating elsewhere. For example, the regulations on maximum permitted floor area ratios may be relaxed around stations. Where developers have actually made some contribution to the cost of the system, it is usually for something extra of very particular interest to the developer, for example, in the form of a direct access from the station into an office block. In Toronto, one developer is providing a new bus and subway interchange facility over an existing station as part of a new shopping and office complex.

Where rail systems have been introduced without this planning framework, then there has been very little effect on urban development. For example in San Diego, although developers reported that the trolley was an important factor, there was in fact little evidence of any actual development; any development which takes place is likely to follow the highway rather than the

126

trolley. There may even be a positive disincentive - as in Baltimore, where 65 acres of car park around the station actually inhibits any rail-linked development taking place.

In the systems visited, there were none which depended on urban development for their success. However, some of the recent extensions depend much more heavily on the possibilities for future development around the line. Unfortunately, some of the extensions were conceived as serving major new public developments and some of these have not been implemented. This illustrates the difficulty of phasing major transport and other developments together when they are funded by different agencies.

8.5.3   Rapid transit enhances current trends in land use

The consensus of opinion on the effects of rapid transit on urban development is that even with the best systems, development can only be successfully channelled if there is a demand for property. Rapid transit can be a contributory factor, but it does not of itself create developments or (in the short term) changes in the urban form.

Rapid transit tends to accentuate existing trends. If an area is undergoing an expansion or boom period, rapid transit can accelerate the expansion. If an area is declining, rapid transit may help to stabilise the area but will not reverse the decline. In one or two examples, the symbiotic process has worked in reverse: in Lille the Metro enabled people in the declining areas to go somewhere else to shop or work, and in Calgary sites which had been earmarked for planned development around stations were left undeveloped and were used as parking lots giving car an advantage over rail.

Development occurs around rail lines and stations when conditions are favourable - that is, when economic conditions favour growth anyway, that growth can be induced to take place around a rail line. For example, the interfacing of office blocks with the subway in Montreal has been very successful, and has also resulted in a direct return on investment by the developer.

Wherever a system has been successful, there is always a variety of other factors which have contributed. Usually these amount to a great deal of public will and money to harness the benefits of the rapid transit system. Developers rarely, if ever, do something for nothing. But where the other factors are favourable, and there is confidence that a line is actually going to be built, development can start to happen even before the line opens, as in Lyon and Marseille.

8.5.4   The effects on the city centre

In looking for effects of a new rapid transit system on urban development, the intuitive expectation is that there will be new areas outside the city which will be opened up by the system and will experience a boom in development. Indeed, some of the systems were specifically intended to do this, and examples of out-of-town developments of this type were found in many of the cities studied in this report.

However, a consistent finding from nearly all the cities was that the rapid transit system encouraged urban development in the city centre. This ties in with the remarks above about reinforcing existing trends; if a city is prospering it is likely to be the central area where the greatest prosperity occurs. The city centre is also the area where a new development is most accessible for the greatest number of people, and a new rail line will increase that accessibility.

A further point favouring the city centre is the motive behind urban development. Developers look for profit from their investments in the form of rents or sales from new offices, shops and factories, and there is less risk attached to development on scarce high value sites such as in the city centre. Access to a rail line can increase the return on investment, but if for any reason the construction of the line does not take place as planned or the patronage does not match expectations, the developer is still assured of a return. The economic viability of an out-of-town development can be poorer and with higher risk than for a development in the downtown area. Rents which can be charged by a developer are normally lower, which may lead to lower profitability. In such cases, the benefits to a developer of access to a rapid transit station are more marginal, and other factors such as highway access, which is often much easier to provide than in the city centre, become at least as important.

Perhaps the clearest example of the effect on the city centre is in Atlanta, where there is intense development taking place in the downtown area as a result of the central plan for the city which proposed development zones around each station on the North-South line. Toronto is world famous for the high rise development which has sprung up along the line. Although much of this is outside the traditional downtown area, the rapid outward expansion of the city and intense pressure for city based employment has created internal mini-downtown areas around the subway stations. These areas are ideal for smaller businesses supporting the large national and international headquarters based in the city centre, as they offer cheaper premises with good access to the city.

It cannot be said, though, that the rapid transit system actually causes the rapid development of these city centres; these are rapidly developing cities in any case and the rapid transit system both feeds on and fuels that growth. For example, Atlanta has established itself as a regional centre for the whole of the Southern States. It is therefore more likely that the rail systems are only one factor affecting the developments, and only serve to intensify a process which would have taken place anyway.

In other cities the effects in the city centres are less clear-cut, though taken together they amount to significant evidence of an influence of the rapid transit system on urban development. In San Diego, the trolley was quoted by developers as a factor to be emphasised in marketing properties. In Grenoble, Nantes and Lyon shopping in the city centre has increased, with some new shops being constructed; in Lyon this was believed to have led to an actual increase in the extent of the city centre itself (at the expense of inner suburban shops). In Lille there has been some growth in city centre development as a result of the pedestrianisation and an alleged reduction in traffic following the opening of the Metro, and in the German cities there have been redevelopment programmes as part of the transport improvements.

New rapid transit systems, especially Light Rail or tramways, can make the city centre more attractive, if the centre is pedestrianised so that people can walk about unhindered by traffic. The benefits come, of course, mainly from pedestrianisation and traffic restraint measures, but it is the installation of a rail system which makes it possible, or at least acceptable, to take these measures. The centres of Lyon, Grenoble, Nantes and some German cities have been made very pleasant places in this way, and in Sacramento environmental improvements were one of the major objectives of the system. In Lille and Marseille, where only small scale pedestrianisation was undertaken, the effects are minor. In Grenoble, and to a lesser extent in Nantes, the presence of attractive-looking, modern trams enhances the appearance of the city centre. However, the cost of enhancing the urban environment in Grenoble was high; the Grenoble tramway cost twice as much as one without any urban enhancement.

8.5.5   Development effects away from the city centres

In some US cities, positive steps have been taken to encourage development at Metro stations. In Washington, for example, "air rights" were sold at stations enabling developers to construct new facilities which were well served by the Metro. In Atlanta, development zones were established around stations on the Northern line which have resulted in the extension of the CBD northwards and the development of office and shopping centres at Brookhaven and Lenox.

Development also occurs around other stations and areas served by the lines where conditions are favourable, for example in Washington where the Silver Springs development takes advantage of Metro access, and at Alexandria which developed rapidly after the extension of the Metro to the suburb. However, the Silver Springs station did not initially attract developers, and when a development was constructed, it was not possible to agree on a joint development. Once development started, other new buildings followed rapidly and land prices increased, illustrating the fact that a market had been created for that site.

In the French cities there are a number of examples of urban development taking place along the Metro or tramway lines - expansion at La Rose in Marseille, at Gorge de Loup and along Line D in Lyon, in Villeneuve d'Ascq in Lille, in Fontaine in Grenoble, at Bellevue, Manufacture and Médiathèque in Nantes. There is evidence of increased building in Marseille and Nantes, and purchases in anticipation of the Metro in Lyon. In each case it is possible to say that the rail line was a contributing, but not the only, factor. Other factors, such as the proximity of highways, the coming of the TGV, or the availability of large sites for redevelopment, are probably more important.

The instances of ribbon development in Hamburg and Munich, and the short-lived shopping boom in the Sudstadt area of Nuremberg when the Metro temporarily terminated there, also bear witness to the effects of a rail system.

Most of these examples are cases where a large development was planned centrally. Where there was no such central plan, little effect is seen, as in Baltimore and Lille.

There is considerable evidence from the systems studied that where rail is introduced into an area which is developing rapidly, it can enhance that boom. The following examples are areas where new shopping or residential developments were taking place and where the coming of the rail system is believed to have contributed to the general prosperity: the Alexandria area of Washington, the Brookhaven and Lenox developments in Atlanta, the downtown suburbs development in San Diego, the new town of Villeneuve d'Ascq in Lille, shopping centres in Nantes, the Europole development in Grenoble, and the City Nord in Hamburg. In San Francisco, BART did not appear to significantly affect the decisions of businesses to locate in the Bay Area

(McDonald & Grefe Inc, 1978). However, BART may well have been one of several factors contributing to the generally positive impact that attracted business to the Bay Area.

There are exceptions to the trend: in Sacramento the only development has occurred in the downtown area, and in Lyon the trend towards suburban shopping was reversed as more people used Metro to the city centre. The economic viability of an out of town development is often much poorer than for a development in the downtown area. Rents which can be charged by a developer are normally lower and highway access is often much easier to provide than in the city centre. In such cases the benefits to a developer of access to a rapid transit station are more marginal.

In areas which are in economic decline, a new Metro or tramway does little. In the run-down Hellemmes area of Lille, there is no evidence of redevelopment even 5 years after the Metro opened. The attempt to create development zones at each station in Lille was counter-productive; it had the effect of freezing development instead. Along the east-west line in Atlanta, there has been no effect on the poorer areas. In Baltimore the Owings Mill development was not very successful, and in Sacramento there was little effect.

A TRRL study of the Tyne and Wear Metro found similar effects (The Metro Report 1986). The demand for industrial property in the early 1980s was low, and Metro had no significant effect on locational decisions. Metro was considered to have had no discernible effect on the locational pattern of new office development, although improved access by public transport did encourage some corporate tenants to retain central area floorspace.

8.5.6   The effect of construction cost and type

Reducing the cost of the construction of a tramway can in itself reduce the possible impact. One way of reducing the cost (which would be employed by many of the proposed British schemes) is to use an existing right of way such as a disused rail line, as in Edmonton. This has both advantages and disadvantages. On the one hand, construction is cheaper and causes less disturbance than construction on a new alignment. Land adjacent to a disused railway may also be ripe for development which could be sparked off by the new line. On the other hand, a disused railway may be hidden away from the main centres, often running along the backs of factories and offices which face a main road, and therefore has less potential both for passengers and development.

Similarly, running a tramway along a major highway, as in San Diego or Calgary, may reduce the impact, since it would then lose much of its speed advantage over car, though this could be outweighed by better access in the city centre.

On the other hand, deciding to go underground has serious implications on cost and also on the speed of construction; here, the Edmonton system suffered as compared with the superficially similar tramway in Calgary. Underground railways also provide poorer access for passengers than tramways, especially if the tunnels are forced to run deep under all the existing services. Putting the line in tunnel can also be an expression of the unwillingness of a city to accept the changes to road layouts and buildings which will be needed in order to incorporate a surface light rail system into the city. In between, there are measures which can be used to enhance the development potential of a tramway, such as traffic restraints, putting tramways through city centre streets and pedestrianisation, as in Grenoble and Nantes.

8.5.7   Public developments

Although effects of rapid transit on urban development have been observed, as noted in previous sections, many developments turn out to be public sector ones which can be viewed as part of the public commitment to support the rapid transit system. Examples are, in Nantes, the developments at Médiathèque and Manufacture and the sports stadium, and in Marseille, the developments of public housing, an exhibition hall and sports stadium. There is usually no commercial profit attached to such developments. Indeed, in many cities the authorities make a conscious effort to take advantage of their new rail systems in planning new public developments, even where these were not planned as an integral part of the rail construction.

A high degree of public investment focused along the line can obscure the effect on private development, which may occur on a smaller scale and in different areas. There can, though, be a multiplier effect as a boom in public or planned development causes the rise in prices which induce private development to follow.

8.5.8   Effect on house prices and construction

The effect of rapid transit on house prices is difficult to determine, and any effect cannot definitely be ascribed to the rail system. Furthermore, there is little data on which to base any conclusions, because studies have been made in only a few cities.

In Washington, examination of housing sales along the metro route showed that homes near stations were appreciating at a faster rate than similar homes further away - at Huntington, by 100 per cent over 5 years compared to 50 per cent for similar houses further away, and at Brookland, by 82 per cent between 1977 and 1979 compared with 31 per cent further away. Prices tended to increase when the line was announced, when construction began, and when service started. The rate of increase was greatest in areas that had potential for improvement or gentrification anyway, or in areas close to downtown Washington. However, an article in the Washington Post in 1980 concluded: "While property prices around some Metro stops may be taking off faster than property around others, one fact bears noting: there is not one stop where prices are not going up."

In Marseille, on the other hand, in the first year of Metro there was no detectable difference between prices for housing near to and remote from Metro. These findings were confirmed in a more recent study (quoted in Tulasne 1989) of property values in the periphery of Marseille, where Metro did not emerge as a significant factor. However, there was some evidence that construction anticipated the coming of the Metro, with more housing constructions in the northeast prior to and at the time of the opening of Line 1, and in the north prior to the opening of Line 2.

In Nantes there was a similar finding, with a very significant sharp increase in construction permits between 1983 and 1986 along the tramway corridor, while permits in the city as a whole remained steady. The conclusion is that there is positive evidence of housing developments taking place preferentially in the tramway corridor prior to and immediately following the opening.

In Tyne and Wear, a study of the housing market revealed that the Metro had a localised effect in a few inner urban areas, where the attractiveness of housing increased and some redevelopment took place. Metro also helped consolidate the attractiveness of outer residential developments. A study of "matched pairs" of houses revealed that, beginning a few months before the opening of the relevant section of line, properties near to Metro stations gained and maintained a slightly higher value compared with properties further away.

9 Some lessons for rapid transit proposals in Britain

9.1 The purpose of this section

In a sense, the whole of the report, especially the Conclusion section, refers to the lessons which can be drawn for rapid transit in Britain. The function of this section, therefore, is simply to highlight some important features which may affect the application of the lessons from abroad.

It is not the function of this report to draw conclusions as to whether the proposed British rapid transit systems would be viable; that would require a detailed study of the proposals and is in any case for others to decide. Some general points can however be made.

9.2 Types of funding

Earlier sections have highlighted the importance of a promoter being able to demonstrate confidence in a scheme by ensuring that adequate funding is available. One such source of funds is passenger revenues, and if revenues can be expected to cover operating costs and provide an adequate return on investment then funding for capital costs should be forthcoming. With most systems abroad, however, local authorities provide subsidies.

The importance of the funding mechanism rests not in the source of funds but in confidence that funds will be available in the future. Experience from the systems visited suggests that property developers need a high level of local or national commitment to a scheme to encourage them to risk investment in development opportunities. As far as contributions to the system itself are concerned, if developers can see that their contribution will make construction more likely, they will be more willing to participate. As an example, Greater Manchester has now received approval for a 50 per cent capital grant from the government, and confidence in the possibilities for funding for a number of other schemes is rising. As a result, there are encouraging signs that developers are interested in participating in some schemes, including extensions in Manchester. On the other hand, if developers believe that the scheme will proceed whether they contribute or not, there may be no incentive for them to do so.

As far as operating costs are concerned, all countries expect to cover as much as possible from revenues, though most countries abroad pay some subsidy. Although in many cases this comes from sales or payroll taxes earmarked for public transport, earmarked taxes are not essential for the success of a rail system: not every US city depends on sales taxes, and there is no equivalent in Canada. Furthermore, it is important to note that, as described in section 4.2.4, readily available subsidies - particularly earmarked taxes - also have disadvantages in that they can lead to a lack of incentives, inefficiency and distortion of the travel market. Earmarked taxes have no equivalent in Britain and it would require a fundamental change in the taxation system to introduce them.

In Britain, public transport as a whole requires a lower level of subsidy than in other countries - some 85percent of bus mileage is operated without subsidy, and subsidies for remaining bus services are decided by competitive tender. Since new rapid transit systems are likely to be in competition with local bus services, local authorities might be charged with unfair competition if they provided a subsidy. Indeed the new guidelines for government grant state that it is unlikely that grant would be awarded to any rapid transit system which was not expected to make an operating profit.

9.3   Costs and revenues

In Britain, public transport generally covers a higher percentage of its operating costs than in France or North America. Even before deregulation, bus services in the major cities typically achieved revenue:cost ratios of 70 per cent, and only in the most highly subsidised were ratios as low as the systems abroad.

Prior to deregulation, the Tyne and Wear Metro was part of the integrated public transport system and so was subsidised out of revenue support. Total revenues from bus and Metro covered about 70 per cent of the costs. Following deregulation, the Metro is still operated by the Passenger Transport Executive and it currently covers 84 per cent of its direct operating costs.

It would, of course, take a detailed study of revenue and cost forecasts to determine whether British rapid transit systems could earn an operating surplus. However, given that most public transport networks abroad have improved their revenue:operating cost ratio after installing rapid transit, there would appear to be some prospect of British systems coming at least as close to covering their operating costs as local bus services.

9.4   Patronage

British cities tend to have population densities about half those in France. Patronage on the major transport corridors is therefore correspondingly less. This helps to explain why cities such as Manchester and Sheffield, although they are bigger than Lyon or Marseille, have survived without a metro system, and are now opting for the light rail option (though finance, and in Manchester the presence of a suburban rail system, are other reasons).

This might imply that achieving the required patronage for profitability might be more difficult in Britain. Working against this conclusion is the fact that the use of public transport per capita in Britain is traditionally higher.

Some of the British proposals include lines which do not at present constitute public transport corridors, in some cases crossing areas which at present are virtually devoid of people. Such systems obviously have to be assessed much more carefully, as their patronage will be determined solely by the success of the property developments. Experience from the systems visited would suggest that, even where property developments do occur, considerable efforts are still required to interface new developments in such a way as to produce the maximum patronage for the rapid transit system.

9.5   The effect of deregulation

Most cities abroad have integrated transport systems, with bus services complementing the Metro or tramway and a common fare scale. While this generally favours the rail mode, by transferring passengers from bus services, the revenue received from passengers for journeys involving a transfer is reduced as it is shared between the bus and rail modes. In Britain, where bus services are deregulated, it is likely that any rapid transit system will find itself in competition with parallel bus services, especially if the fares are higher (as the current guidelines for assessment suggest they might be, if this is required to minimise the subsidy requirement). The Manchester Metro proposal was reassessed in the light of deregulation and was found to still be viable. In other systems, the effect of competition with bus services may be greater and this now needs to be taken into consideration. It could be argued that if a bus system is able to compete successfully, the case for rapid transit must be weak anyway, especially as it will inevitably cost a great deal more than a bus system.

9.6   Environmental effects

The pleasant ambience in cities with Metro or tramway systems has been remarked on already. The effect in Nantes, Grenoble and Lyon has only been achieved by extensive pedestrianisation and planning of the city centre. In Lille and Marseille, few environmental measures were taken and there was a much smaller effect on the ambience.

However, the cost of environmental measures is high. In the case of Grenoble, the relocation of frontages, the redesign of the main line station, noise and vibration reduction and other measures to incorporate the tramway into the city fabric added half as much again to the basic cost of the tramway. It seems unlikely that the operators of new British systems will be able to provide such environmental improvements on a similar scale. In common with public authorities abroad, British local authorities are likely to face pressure to introduce these improvements from public funds.

9.7   Urban development

The importance of central planning in providing the climate under which development can take place has already been noted. It should be mentioned that this was also a factor in the success of the London Docklands Light Railway, which was installed as part of the overall redevelopment plan under a Development Corporation. In Tyne and Wear, the introduction of Enterprise Zones and, more recently, an Urban Development Corporation have been successful in attracting new development. However, as neither are related to the Metro, little, if any, new development has been built around the line.

A principal conclusion from this report must be that development is much more likely to follow the British rapid transit systems if some comprehensive plan is followed or development is otherwise encouraged to take place. If it is left to developers to provide the spur without incentives, there is a risk that nothing will happen until the new line has been in place for ten or twenty years. But if developers can have confidence that the system will actually be built, they are more likely to be interested in developing and in contributing to the funding. This could take the form of paying for the parts of the system such as extensions or connections to stations, or the building of the system could be conditional on the outcome of negotiations regarding developer contributions.

There are many different types of planning regimes. The least successful are those without any positive development powers, for such authorities can do little to make things happen. The most successful in terms of rapid transit will be those that have similar powers (and money) to those of the current development corporations. There also need to be supporting policies to limit development elsewhere.

10 Acknowledgements

The authors would like to acknowledge the generosity of the many people in the transport organisations and local authorities who were visited during the course of this study, who gave their time and supplied a vast amount of information.

They would also like to acknowledge the contributions made by John Simpson, Tim Hibbitt and Marie Woolley to the analysis and text, and by Linda Lines and Pat Perrin in preparing the final version of the text.

The work described in this report forms part of the research programme of the former Transport Planning Division (Division Head: Dr W S Clough) of the Safety and Transportation Group of TRRL.

11 References

11.1 General

DICKINS I (1988). An Introduction to Light Rail Transit in Europe. Department of Planning and Landscape, Birmingham Polytechnic, Departmental Working Paper 32.

DUNN J A Jr (1980). Coordination of Urban Transit Services: The German Model. Transportation 9 (1980), 33-43.

GRIECO M S (1988). Literature Review: The Impact of Transport Investment Projects Upon the Inner City. For the Department of the Environment: Inner Cities Directorate. Transport Studies Unit, University of Oxford.

GOLDSACK P J (1980). Rail Transit Construction around the World. Transportation 9 (1980), 83-92.

HALCROW FOX AND ASSOCIATES (1989). Mass Rapid Transit in Developing Countries. Study carried out for the Overseas Unit of TRRL (Halcrow Fox and Associates, 1989).

PUCHER J (1988). Urban public transport subsidies in Western Europe and North America. Transportation Quarterly, 42, 377-402.

SIMPSON B J (1987a). Planning and public transport in Great Britain, France and West Germany. Longman, London and New York.

SIMPSON B J (1988a). City centre planning and public transport: case studies from Britain, West Germany and France. Van Nostrand Reinhold.

SIMPSON B J (1989). Urban Rail Transit - an appraisal. TRRL Contractor Report CR 140. Transport and Road Research Laboratory, Crowthorne.

SIMPSON B J (1990). Urban Rail Transit: costs and funding. TRRL Contractor Report CR 160. Transport and Road Research Laboratory, Crowthorne.

TRANSPORTATION RESEARCH BOARD (1989). Light Rail Transit - New System Successes at Affordable Prices. Special Report 221. National Research Council, Washington DC.

WRIGHT A A. Urban Transit Systems. Guidelines for Examining Options. World Bank Technical Paper 52.

11.2 Great Britain

DEPARTMENT OF TRANSPORT (1989a). Provisional guidance note on the Highway and Vehicle engineering aspects of street-running light rapid transit systems.

DEPARTMENT OF TRANSPORT (1989b). Circular. Section 56 Grant for Public Transport. HMSO London.

DEPARTMENT OF TRANSPORT (1989c). Transport Statistics Great Britain (1978-1988). HMSO London.

KOMPFNER P (1979). Notes on Light Rail Transit in Great Britain. Transport and Road Research Laboratory supplementary report 482. Department of Transport, Crowthorne.

MINISTRY OF TRANSPORT (1968). The Transport Act 1968, ch 73. HMSO London.

PICKETT M W and PERRETT K E (1984). The effect of the Tyne and Wear Metro on residential property values, Transport and Road Research Laboratory supplementary report 825, Department of the Environment/Department of Transport, Crowthorne.

METRO MONITORING AND DEVELOPMENT STUDY (Transport and Road Research Laboratory, University of Newcastle-Upon-Tyne, Tyne and Wear County Council, Tyne and Wear Passenger Transport Executive (1986). The Metro Report: The impact of Metro and public transport integration in Tyne and Wear.

11.3 France

11.3.1   France: General

CENTRE D'ETUDES DES TRANSPORTS URBAINS, for Ministère de l'Equipement, du Logement, de l'Aménagement du Territoire et des Transports. (1988). Villes et Déplacements. CETUR, 8 avenue Aristide Briand, 92220 Bagneux, France.

INTERNATIONAL RAILWAY JOURNAL (1986). A Hive of Activity in French Cities. IRJ, December 1986.

INTERNATIONAL RAILWAY JOURNAL (1989). France: Healthy Growth in RT. IRJ, August 1989.

MARCHAND B, SANDERS L AND OFFNER J-M (1983). Les effets d'une nouvelle station de métro sur le commerce avoisinant. TEC No 58, May-June 1983.

MINISTERE DES TRANSPORTS (1988). French Urban Public Transport Equipment. CETUR, 8 avenue Aristide Briand, 92220 Bagneux, France.

MINISTERE DES TRANSPORTS ET DE LA MER (1988). Annuaire Statistique sur les Réseaux de Transport Urbain de Province, Statistiques 1980-1987. CETUR, 8 avenue Aristide Briand, 92220 Bagneux, France.

MITRIC S (1986). Organisation of Urban Public Transport in France: Lessons for Developing Countries. The World Bank, Washington DC, USA.

11.3.2 Marseille

AGENCE D'URBANISME DE L'AGGLOMERATION MARSEILLAISE (1986). Urbanisation et Transports à Marseille - Le Grand Marseille en Chemin?

AGENCE D'URBANISME DE L'AGGLOMERATION MARSEILLAISE (1986). Marseilles and its Development, Directing Principles of Planification for Tomorrow.

DALMAIS, C and MAZZELLA, P (1985). Métro et Urbanisme. Du suivi à l'anticipation, Agence d'Urbanisme de l'Agglomération Marseillaise.

MINISTERE DE L'ENVIRONNEMENT ET DU CADRE DE VIE - MINISTERE DES TRANSPORTS (1979). Etudes de Suivi des Ouvertures des Métros de Lyon et Marseille, Principaux resultats. CETUR, Département des Etudes Generales, 46 av. Aristide Briand, 92220 Bagneux, France.

OFFICE DE COORDINATION DES TRANSPORTS DE LA CIRCULATION ET DU STATIONNEMENT DE MARSEILLE (1985). Suivi de l'Impact de la Mise en Service de la 2e Ligne de Métro (Joliette-Castellane), du Tramway Modernise et de la Restructuration du Réseau de Surface - Evolution des Statistiques d'Exploitation, Note de Synthèse, Résultats de l'Enquête auprès des Utilisateurs du Métro. Parc Valmer, 271 Corniche J F Kennedy, 13007 Marseille, France.

OFFICE DE COORDINATION DES TRANSPORTS DE LA CIRCULATION ET DU STATIONNEMENT DE MARSEILLE (1985). Enquête auprès des Usagers de la 2e Ligne de Métro, novembre 1984, résultats. Parc Valmer, 271 Corniche J F Kennedy, 13007 Marseille, France.

OFFICE DE COORDINATION DES TRANSPORTS DE LA CIRCULATION ET DU STATIONNEMENT DE MARSEILLE (1979). Impact du Métro un An après, Tomes 1–7 1979. Parc Valmer, 271 Corniche J F Kennedy, 13007 Marseille, France.

SOCIETE DU METRO DE MARSEILLE. Le Métro de Marseille. 44, avenue Alexandre Dumas, 13008 Marseille, France.

SOCIETE DU METRO DE MARSEILLE, ET REGIE DES TRANSPORTS DE MARSEILLE. Le Métro de Marseille, La 2e Ligne. 44, avenue Alexandre Dumas, 13008 Marseille, France.

TULASNE E (1989). Les Effets du Métro à Marseille. AGAM/CEIFICI Working Paper. Agence d'Urbanisme de l'Agglomeration Marseillaise.

11.3.3 Lyon

SOCIETE D'ECONOMIE MIXTE DU METROPOLITAIN DE L'AGGLOMERATION LYONNAISE. Métro Information, No 9 octobre 1979, No 11 janvier 1984, No 12 fevrier 1986, No 13 juin 1988. SEMALY, 25 cours Emile-Zola, 69625 Villeurbanne Cedex, France.

SOCIETE D'ECONOMIE MIXTE DU METROPOLITAIN DE L'AGGLOMERATION LYONNAISE (1981). Le Métro Lyonnais. SEMALY, 25 cours Emile-Zola, 69625 Villeurbanne Cedex, France.

SOCIETE D'ECONOMIE MIXTE DU METROPOLITAIN DE L'AGGLOMERATION LYONNAISE (1983). Etude d'Impact, janvier. SEMALY, 25 cours Emile-Zola, 69625 Villeurbanne Cedex, France.

SOCIETE D'ECONOMIE MIXTE DU METROPOLITAIN DE L'AGGLOMERATION LYONNAISE (1986). Plan de déplacements urbains, Prolongement de la Ligne D Gorge de Loup Gare de Vaise, décembre, 25 cours Emile-Zola, 69625 Villeurbanne Cedex, France.

SOCIETE D'ECONOMIE MIXTE DU METROPOLITAIN DE L'AGGLOMERATION LYONNAISE (1988). Mémento des Caracteristiques Principales du Métro de Lyon. SEMALY, 25 cours Emile-Zola, 69625 Villeurbanne Cedex, France.

SYNDICAT DES TRANSPORTS EN COMMUN DE LA REGION LYONNAISE (1979). Suivi du Métro. Que Pensent les Lyonnais de leur Métro?

SYNDICAT DES TRANSPORTS EN COMMUN DE LA REGION LYONNAISE (1979). Suivi du Métro. Les Usagers du Métro Lyonnais et leurs déplacements.

SYNDICAT DES TRANSPORTS EN COMMUN DE LA REGION LYONNAISE (1983). TCL Rapport d'Activité.

SYNDICAT DES TRANSPORTS EN COMMUN DE LA REGION LYONNAISE (1984). L'Agglomération Lyonnaise et les Transports de Personnes, Mémento Statistique.

SYNDICAT DES TRANSPORTS EN COMMUN DE LA REGION LYONNAISE (1987). Quand le Transport se met en Quatre - SYTRAL, TCL, SEMALY, GIHP.

11.3.4 Lille

CENTRE D'ETUDES DES TRANSPORTS URBAINS, for Ministère de l'Equipement, du Logement, de l'Aménagement du Térritoire et des Transports. (1981).Impact de la Ligne No 1 du VAL Sur l'Environnement Urbain, Note No 2. CETUR, 8 avenue Aristide Briand, 92220 Bagneux, France.

COMMUNAUTE URBAIN DE LILLE (1985). Les Transports Collectifs dans la Communaute Urbain de Lille. Etude d'Impact de la Ligne No 1 du Métro - Enquête aux Stations du Métro et aux Arrêts du Tramway d'Octobre 1984, Enquête Après Mise en Service du 20me Tronçon, Fonctionnement des Transports Collectifs dans le Centre de Lille.

11.3.5 Nantes

PITREL J (1983). Le Tramway Nantais. TEC No 56, janvier-fevrier.

L'AGENCE D'ETUDES URBAINES DE L'AGGLOMERATION NANTAIS (1984). Album de l'Agglomération Nantais. 110 Bd Michelet, 44300 Nantes, France.

L'AGENCE D'ETUDES URBAINES DE L'AGGLOMERATION NANTAIS (1987). Prospective, Agglomération Nantais. 110 Bd Michelet, 44300 Nantes, France.

L'AGENCE D'ETUDES URBAINES DE L'AGGLOMERATION NANTAIS (1987). Observatoire des Effets du Tramway sur l'Environnement Economique, 20me Partie: Entretiens Auprès des Professionels. 110 Bd Michelet, 44300 Nantes, France.

L'AGENCE D'ETUDES URBAINES DE L'AGGLOMERATION NANTAIS (1988). Article Nantes: Autour du Tramway la Ville Bouge Lentement mais Sûrement. 110 Bd Michelet, 44300 Nantes, France.

SYNDICAT INTERCOMMUNAL A VOCATION MULTIPLE DE L'AGGLOMERATION NANTAIS (1987). TAN j'y suis!. 3 rue Bellier, 44046 Nantes Cedex, France.

11.3.6 Grenoble

AGENCE D'URBANISME DE LA REGION GRENOBLOISE (1986). Special Transports & Déplacements. Les Cahiers de l'AURG. 21 rue Lesdiguières, 38000 Grenoble, France.

AGENCE D'URBANISME DE LA REGION GRENOBLOISE (1988). Les Déplacements Urbains dans l'Agglomération Grenobloise. 21 rue Lesdiguières, 38000 Grenoble, France.

AGENCE D'URBANISME DE LA REGION GRENOBLOISE (1988). Etude de Rabattement des Voitures Particulières Autour de la Station Grand'Place. 21 rue Lesdiguières, 38000 Grenoble, France.

AGENCE D'URBANISME DE LA REGION GRENOBLOISE (1988). Etude de Rabattement des Voitures Particulières sur la Première Ligne de Tramway - Stations de Fontaine. 21 rue Lesdiguières, 38000 Grenoble, France.

LE DAUPHINE LIBÈRE (1989). Enfin Crédible. Le Dauphine Libère, April 1989.

SYNDICAT MIXTE DES TRANSPORTS EN COMMUN DE L'AGGLOMERATION GRENOBLOISE (1983). Dossier Tramway, Compte Rendu des Etudes. Décision de Réalisation, Juin 1983. 3, rue Malakoff, 38000 Grenoble, France.

SYNDICAT MIXTE DES TRANSPORTS EN COMMUN DE L'AGGLOMERATION GRENOBLOISE (1983). Première Ligne de Tramway, Etude d'Impact. 3, rue Malakoff, 38000 Grenoble, France.

SYNDICAT MIXTE DES TRANSPORTS EN COMMUN DE L'AGGLOMERATION GRENOBLOISE (1984). Du Tram... Au Tram... Etude d'Impact: les Principaux Resultats. 3, rue Malakoff, 38000 Grenoble, France.

SYNDICAT MIXTE DES TRANSPORTS EN COMMUN DE L'AGGLOMERATION GRENOBLOISE (1988). Deuxième Ligne de Tramway, Etude d'Impact. 3, rue Malakoff, 38000 Grenoble, France.

SYNDICAT MIXTE DES TRANSPORTS EN COMMUN DE L'AGGLOMERATION GRENOBLOISE (1988). Une ville et un Tramway, Dossier d'information sur la réalisation du Tramway de l'Agglomération Grenobloise. 3, rue Malakoff, 38000 Grenoble, France.

11.3.7   Paris

PREFECTURE DE LA REGION D'ILE-DE-FRANCE (1985). Les Transports de Voyageurs en Ile-de-France, 1985. 21-23 rue Miollis, 75732 Paris Cedex 15, France.

REGIE AUTONOME DES TRANSPORTS PARISIENS (1984). Projet de Rocade Tramway en Site Propre entre Saint-Denis et Bobigny, Dossier d'Enquête Prealable à la Déclaration d'Utilité Publique. 53ter, quai des Grands Augustins 75271 Paris Cedex 06, France.

REGIE AUTONOME DES TRANSPORTS PARISIENS (1985). Saint-Denis-La Courneuve-Drancy-Bobigny, Le Tramway, Une Ligne Nouvelle en Seine-Saint-Denis. 53ter, quai des Grands Augustins 75271 Paris Cedex 06, France.

INTERNATIONAL RAILWAY JOURNAL (1985). RATP tries low-capacity transit system in Paris. IRJ, November 1985.

11.3.8   Strasbourg

D'AUFRESNE MARIE (1989). Bataille strasbourgeoise entre le VAL et le tramway. Le Figaro, June 1989.

11.3.9   Toulouse

RAILWAY GAZETTE INTERNATIONAL (1985). Toulouse follows Lille into full automation. RGI, November 1985.

K

11.4 USA

11.4.1 USA: General

CERVERO R (1984). Rail transit and urban development. J.American Planning Association, 50, 133-47.

DICKINS I (1987). Rapid Transit and Land Use in North America. Department of Planning and Landscape, Birmingham Polytechnic, Departmental Working Paper 22.

DOO H and WEIL R (1976). The Use of Value Capture in Major Mass Transit Projects. Department of Transportation, Washington DC.

GOMEZ-IBANEZ J A (1985). A Dark Side to Light Rail? The Experience of Three New Transit Systems. J.American Planning Association, Summer 1985 337-350.

KNIGHT R L (1980). The Impact of Rail Transit on Land Use: Evidence and a Change of Perspective. Transportation 9 (1980), 3-16.

KNIGHT R L and TRYGG L L (1977). Evidence of Land Use Impacts of Rapid Transit Systems. Transportation 6 (1977), 231-247.

MCLAUGHLIN P V (1989). Integration of Public Transit into Land Use Decisions: US Case Studies. Transport Policy, 11-15 Sept 1989, 185-193.

ORSKI C K (1980). The Federal Rail Transport Policy: Rhetoric or Reality? Transportation 9 (1980), 57-65.

PICKRELL D H (1985). Rising Deficits and the Uses of Transit Subsides in the United States. Journal of Transport Economics and Policy, Sept 1985, 281-298.

PRIEST D E (1980). Enhancing the Developmental Impact of Rail Transit. Transportation 9 (1980), 45-55.

PUCHER J et al (1983). Impacts of subsidies on the costs of urban public transport. Journal of Transport Economics and Policy, 17, 155-76.

PUCHER J and MARKSTEDT A (1983). Consequences of Public Ownership and Subsidies for Mass Transit: Evidence from Case Studies and Regression Analysis. Transportation 11 (1983), 323-345.

PUSHKAREV B S. Urban Rail in America - An Exploration of Criteria for fixed Guideway Transit.

SKINNER R E and DEEN T B (1980). Second Generation US Rail Transit Systems: Prospects and Perils. Transportation 9 (1980), 17-32.

TAYLOR S F (1980). Light Rail Transit in the United States. Transportation 9 (1980), 67-74.

US DEPARTMENT OF TRANSPORTATION (1976). Light Rail Transit - A State of the Art Review Executive Summary.

11.4.2   Washington, DC

DAMM, D, LERMAN, S R, LERNER-LAM, EVA and YOUNG, J (1980). Response of Urban Real Estate Values in Anticipation of the Washington Metro. Journal of Transport Economics and Policy, September, pp315-336.

JHK & ASSOCIATES (1987), for the WASHINGTON METROPOLITAN AREA TRANSIT AUTHORITY. Final Report for the Development-Related Ridership Survey. 600 Fifth Street, N.W., Washington D.C., 20001.

LANGLEY, Dr C J Jr (1981), for the Transportation Research Board. Highways and Property Values: The Washington Beltway Revisited.

LINFORD, A N, BA(Hons), BTP (1988). The Impact of the Washington Metrorail System on Land Development. Midland Metro, West Midlands Passenger Transport Authority, 16 Summer Lane, Birmingham, B19 3SD.

METROPOLITAN WASHINGTON COUNCIL OF GOVERNMENTS (1977). A Strategic Plan for a Metro Before and After Study of the Washington Region: With Detailed Recommendations for a First Two Year Work Program. 1225 Connecticut Avenue, N.W., Washington D.C., USA.

METROPOLITAN WASHINGTON COUNCIL OF GOVERNMENTS (1988). Employment change in the Metropolitan Washington Region (1980-1985). 1225 Connecticut Avenue, N.W., Washington D.C., USA.

RICHARDS, CAROL L (1979), for Metropolitan Washington Council of Governments. More Than a Subway, A Chronicle of Transit Goals for the Nation's Capital. 1225 Connecticut Avenue, N.W., Washington D.C., USA.

TURNER, CARMEN E (1985). WMATA Progress Towards 160km System. Developing Metros, pp71-73.

WASHINGTON METROPOLITAN AREA TRANSIT AUTHORITY (1978). Assessment of Washington Metropolitan Area Rail Rapid Transit System. DOT/TSC-UM929-PM-79-4. 600 Fifth Street, N.W., Washington D.C., 20001, USA.

WASHINGTON METROPOLITAN AREA TRANSIT AUTHORITY (1982). Executed Plan for Stable and Reliable Funding Sources. 600 Fifth Street, N.W., Washington D.C., 20001, USA.

WASHINGTON METROPOLITAN AREA TRANSIT AUTHORITY (1987). Development-Related Ridership Survey - Final Report. 600 Fifth Street, N.W., Washington D.C., 20001, USA.

WASHINGTON METROPOLITAN AREA TRANSIT AUTHORITY (1989). General Manager's Budget, Financial Program and Summaries. 600 Fifth Street, N.W., Washington D.C., 20001, USA.

WASHINGTON METROPOLITAN AREA TRANSIT AUTHORITY (1989). Approved Budget, Capital Improvement Program - FY 1989-FY 1993. 600 Fifth Street, N.W., Washington D.C., 20001, USA.

11.4.3 Baltimore, Maryland

CARTER M M (1987), for Mass Transit Administration. Light Rail Transit Feasibility Study Report. 300 West Lexington Street, Baltimore, Maryland 21201, USA.

MARYLAND DEPARTMENT OF TRANSPORTATION, MASS TRANSIT ADMINIS-TRATION (1988). Environmental Effects Report. 300 West Lexington Street, Baltimore, Maryland 21201, USA.

MARYLAND DEPARTMENT OF TRANSPORTATION, MASS TRANSIT ADMINIS-TRATION (1987). The Central Corridor Light Rail Project. Innovation and Affordability in Expanding the Baltimore Metropolitan Transit System. 300 West Lexington Street, Baltimore, Maryland 21201, USA.

U.S. DEPARTMENT OF TRANSPORTATION, URBAN MASS TRANSIT ADMINIS-TRATION and the MARYLAND DEPARTMENT OF TRANSPORTATION, MASS TRANSIT ADMINISTRATION (1987). Northeast Extension of the Baltimore Metro. Final Environmental Impact Statement. 300 West Lexington Street, Baltimore, Maryland 21201, USA.

11.4.4 Atlanta, Georgia

ATLANTA REGIONAL COMMISSION (1978). Transit Impact Monitoring Program, Results of East Line Pilot Project, 1970-1976.

DAVIS, E L (1986). MARTA: A Stimulant to Atlanta Development? Transportation Planning and Technology, Vol 10, pp241-256.

MAC, I (1982). Atlanta and Transportation: Entering the New Decade. ITE Journal, April, pp33-36.

METROPOLITAN ATLANTA RAPID TRANSIT AUTHORITY (1987). Division of Service Planning and Scheduling. 1985 On-Board Survey Report. 401 West Peachtree Street NE, Suite 2200, Atlanta, Georgia 30365.

POTTER, P E (1979). Urban Restructuring: One Goal of the New Atlanta Transit System. Traffic Quarterly, January, pp45-60.

11.4.5   San Diego, California

METROPOLITAN TRANSIT DEVELOPMENT BOARD. Progress: 1976-1986. 620 "C" Street, Suite 400, San Diego, California 92101.

METROPOLITAN TRANSIT DEVELOPMENT BOARD (1984). East Urban Corridor, Alternatives Analysis/Environmental Impact Statement. 620 "C" Street, Suite 400, San Diego, California 92101, USA.

METROPOLITAN TRANSIT DEVELOPMENT BOARD (1986). East Urban Corridor, Final Environmental Impact Statement. 620 "C" Street, Suite 400, San Diego, California 92101, USA.

METROPOLITAN TRANSIT DEVELOPMENT BOARD (1989). Mid-Coast Corridor, Transit System Planning Study. 620 "C" Street, Suite 400, San Diego, California 92101, USA.

QUINTIN W P Jr (1987), for the Metropolitan Transit Development Board. Signalling the San Diego Trolley. 620 "C" Street, Suite 400, San Diego, California 92101, USA.

SAN DIEGO ASSOCIATION OF GOVERNMENTS (1989), for the Metropolitan Transit Development Board. Euclid Trolley Line Corridor Study. 620 "C" Street, Suite 400, San Diego, California 92101, USA.

SAN DIEGO ASSOCIATION OF GOVERNMENTS (1984). San Diego Trolley - The First Three Years. 1200 Third Avenue, Suite 524, Security Pacific Plaza, San Diego, California 92101, USA.

11.4.6   Sacramento, California

JOHNSTON R A, SPERLING D, DELUCHI M A and TRACY S (1988). Transportation Research - A, Vol 21A, No.6, pp459-475.

SACRAMENTO REGIONAL TRANSIT (1987). Design Guidelines for Bus and Light Rail Facilities. PO Box 2110, Sacramento, California, 95812-2110, USA.

SACRAMENTO REGIONAL TRANSIT (1988). Standard Operating Procedure, Development Within One-Quarter Mile of Light Rail Stations. PO Box 2110, Sacramento, California, 95812-2110, USA.

TAPLIN M R(1987). The Sacramento Light Rail Story. Modern Tramway, November, pp376-381.

11.4.6 San Francisco

US DEPARTMENT OF TRANSPORTATION, US DEPARTMENT OF HOUSING AND URBAN DEVELOPMENT (1979a). BART in the San Francisco Bay Area- The Final Report of the BART Impact Program.

US DEPARTMENT OF TRANSPORTATION, US DEPARTMENT OF HOUSING AND URBAN DEVELOPMENT (1979b). The Economic and Financial Impacts of BART - Final Report.

11.5 Canada

11.5.1 Canada: General

SULLIVAN B E (1980). Light Rail Transit in Canada. Transportation 9 (1980), 75-82.

11.5.2 Calgary and Edmonton, Alberta

ALBERTA TRANSPORTATION AND UTILITIES (1988). Urban Transportation Branch. Alberta Cities Transportation Partnership. 1st Floor, 4999 - 98 Avenue, Edmonton, Alberta T6B 2X3, Canada.

ALBERTA TRANSPORTATION AND UTILITIES (1988). Annual Report 1987/88. 1st Floor, 4999 - 98 Avenue, Edmonton, Alberta T6B 2X3.

CERVERO, R (1985). A tale of two cities: light rapid transit in Canada. J. Transportation Engineering, 111, 633-50.

CITY OF CALGARY (1984). LRT South Corridor Impact Monitoring Study, Land Use and Development Trends, Summary Report (1979-1983).

CITY OF CALGARY (1989). Northwest LRT Impact Monitoring Study Volume 2: Appendices to the Background Report.

Railway Gazette International (1986). Alberta Twins Push on with Light Rail. RGI, Aug 1986, 576-577.

11.5.3 Montreal, Quebec

COMMUNAUTE URBAIN DE MONTREAL (1983). The Montreal Metro.

MINISTERE DES TRANSPORTS DE QUEBEC (1988). Transportation in the Montreal Region - 1988-1989 Plan of Action - Summary. 700 boul. Saint-Cyrille Est, Quebec.

11.5.4 Toronto, Ontario

TORONTO TRANSIT COMMISSION (1987). Annual Report. 1900 Yonge St, Toronto M4S 1Z2.

TORONTO TRANSIT COMMISSION (1987). Metropolitan Toronto: The Transit/Development Connection. 1900 Yonge St, Toronto M4S 1Z2.

Index

151

Printed in the United Kingdon by HMSO, Edinburgh Press
Dd 294506 C10 8/92 3397/4 19593 Ed(204301)